World War II
Scottish Tales of Adventure

Allan Burnett is one of Scotland's best-selling authors for young readers. He was born and brought up in the Western Isles and educated at the University of Edinburgh, while working after dark as a ghost-tour guide. Among Allan's other books are *William Wallace and All That* and *Invented in Scotland: Scottish Ingenuity and Invention throughout the Ages.*

World War II

Scottish Tales of Adventure

Allan Burnett

BIRLINN

In memory of Willie Ritchie DFM

First published in 2011 by
Birlinn Limited
West Newington House
10 Newington Road
Edinburgh
EH9 1QS

www.birlinn.co.uk

ISBN 978 1 84158 933 6
eBook ISBN 978 0 85790 064 7

British Library Cataloguing-in-Publication Data
A catalogue record for this book is available from the British Library

Typeset by Iolaire Typesetting, Newtonmore
Printed and bound by 🐾 Grafica Veneta S.P.A., Italy

Contents

Introduction

This is a book about war. That doesn't mean it is all guns blazing, and nothing else. There is a lot more to a good war story than bombs and machine guns – although you will find plenty of both in this book.

A good war story might have no weapons in it at all. Instead of being packed with explosions, it is bursting with emotion. The characters' thoughts and feelings are what drive the story forward, and capture our hearts.

Many people had their hearts in their mouths when war was declared. There were no bombs, no machine guns and no explosions. Just a crackling voice on a wireless radio set that made everybody freeze.

'This country is at war with Germany,' said the voice. It was the British Prime Minister, Neville Chamberlain.

People never forgot where they were or what they were doing when they heard those words just after 11 o'clock in the morning on 3 September 1939. Some were in their living rooms. Others were out walking the dog, and rushed back to hear the news. Many were at church. It was a Sunday, after all.

That was back in the days when Sunday was still holy – a day for peace and quiet. Except Sunday, 3 September 1939, created the opposite of peace and quiet. It created World War II – or the Second World War, to give it its Sunday name.

World War II sometimes sounds like a Bible story – a battle between good and evil. Or, as American soldiers said at the time, it was the good guys versus the bad guys.

The good guys were the British and their supporters – known as the Allies. The bad guys were Nazi Germany and their supporters – known as the Axis Powers.

Whose side would you have been on? The answer might seem obvious. Nazi Germany led by Adolf Hitler tried to conquer the world, and kill everyone they didn't like. Millions of people died as a result. There is no doubt they were the bad guys.

Except, for people who lived through the war, it was sometimes not so easy to tell the good side from the bad. In this book you will discover people who were on the German side, but turned out not to be such bad people after all.

The stories here also reveal that the so-called good guys could sometimes treat people in a way that was really cruel and barbaric. So things were often not very clear-cut.

It can be hard to tell our enemy from our friend sometimes, and some of the stories here invite us to see ourselves through our enemy's eyes, to feel things our enemy is feeling.

Maybe if we can see things from an enemy's point of view, it will help us work things out peacefully. On the other hand, these tales show that we human beings are a warlike bunch, and we are fascinated by struggles, battles and conflicts.

There have been plenty of battles in Scotland's long history. This book looks at World War II from a Scottish point of view, because this small country played a big part in the war – even though most of the battles were in foreign lands.

The stories here are about men and women, allies and enemies. Some were born in Scotland, some were not – but they all had 'a Scottish war'.

So what exactly does it mean to have had 'a Scottish war'? Read on and find out.

CHAPTER 1

A Long Minute

Lance-Sergeant Stewart Watson opened his eyes. He wondered how long he had been unconscious. He also wondered why everything was upside down.

Bruised and bleeding, Watson's body was slung over another man's shoulders. His head and arms swayed gently from side to side as his bearer plodded along.

Watson looked down at the legs of the soldier carrying him. That's an enemy uniform, Watson thought to himself with alarm. What's going to happen to me?

There were other thoughts, too. Where am I? How did I get here? How badly wounded am I?

It was the summer of 1944. Watson had been fighting in a battle at a French town called Caen. Watson was in the Glasgow Highlanders. They were a Scottish regiment of the British Army. They were fighting on the Allied side against the enemy – the German army.

Caen was a beautiful medieval town of old churches and

market squares. It was in a place called Normandy, in north-west France. Caen was an important town during the war. Whoever controlled Caen could control the roads and rivers around it.

As Sergeant Watson was carried along by the German soldier, he felt a sharp pain in his arm. It was a bad wound. He remembered crossing his own front line and going into no-man's-land – the danger zone. Then he had been hit by an explosion and passed out. Now he realised he was still on the battlefield, which was somewhere on the outskirts of Caen.

Up until now, the town had been in the hands of the Germans. The Allies were determined to drive the Germans out and seize it. The Allies had landed on nearby beaches on D-Day and then come here. The success of the war depended on what happened next.

It was all a long way from Watson's home in Maryhill, Glasgow. He wondered if he would ever get back there. Would he ever see his family again? Or his girlfriend? Would he ever see the River Clyde? Before the war he had worked on the river as an apprentice in a shipyard.

There was hope. Watson realised the German soldier was actually carrying him towards the Allied front line. He could tell the German was wounded, too. Now the enemy soldier wanted to give himself up – and save Watson's life.

Eventually they reached safety. The two men were picked up by other soldiers from the Allied side. Watson was pleased to see that the brave German seemed to be getting the same care and attention as he was. Both men were put on stretchers and carried back to base.

Watson was now safely behind Allied lines, but his life was still in danger. Without treatment for his wounds he could die. At the base camp, trenches had been dug in the soil where wounded soldiers were laid while they waited to be taken to hospital. Watson and his new German companion were lowered into a trench.

This was a scary time. If a soldier passed out and died while lying in the trench, the other soldiers just covered him up with soil and buried him there. Luckily, Watson and the German soldier managed to hang on. They were taken away in an ambulance by a Red Cross nurse.

'Do you know what has happened to my brother?' the nurse asked Watson. 'He is a soldier fighting in Caen.'

Watson shook his head. 'Sorry, I don't,' he said grimly.

An RAF aeroplane was waiting for Watson and his new German companion. It flew them from France to England. 'We're on our way back to Blighty!' said Watson with a cheer. The flight home gave everyone time to think private thoughts while the plane's engines and propellers roared.

The serious wound in Watson's arm was a painful reminder of the battle he had left behind. How were his men getting on without him? As a Lance-Sergeant, he had an important duty to the men under his command. In fact, it was while doing his duty that he got himself injured.

Watson recalled the events before the explosion. He and his platoon had been advancing across farmland outside Caen. They were in a cornfield on the edge of a forest. The battle was very bloody. Bullets were whizzing everywhere. There were explosions as artillery shells pounded the soil near and far.

One of the men was struck down in the crossfire. Watson was

nearby and went to his aid. He dragged the wounded man into a tank dugout. This sheltered spot had been used to protect an enemy German tank before the Allied advance forced the Germans back. Now the dugout was being used as a makeshift first-aid station.

Watson and his comrade were pinned down by enemy fire. If anyone popped his head above the tops of the corn he would be shot. While Watson scanned the ground looking for a way out, he noticed something sticking out of the soil. He wriggled out a little to take a look at it.

It was a human hand.

Judging by the civilian clothing on the arm, this might have been the farmer of the cornfield. Once he had peacefully tended these fields. Now he was dead and buried.

Back in the dugout, Watson turned to the stricken soldier. 'You'll have to hang on a minute,' said Watson. 'I'm going to get help. I'll not be long.'

Before leaving, Watson said again: 'Just hang on a minute.'

As soon as there was a lull in the gunfire, Watson was off. Crawling on his belly. Then padding with his back bent and head down low. Then running at full pelt.

The battle had moved on. Where were the rest of his men? He raced down the side of the forest. He looked for a shortcut to base camp and ran across a stream. Then a wave of bombs started dropping.

All of a sudden, Lance-Sergeant Watson was in oblivion. He felt like he had been blasted to kingdom come.

'Just a minute . . .' This was the promise he had made to the wounded man in the dugout, but there would be no going back now. He lost conciousness and everything went dark.

Then, by some miracle, he was rescued by the German soldier. Now he was on the RAF plane, on his way home. It was all very strange and unexpected.

When the plane landed, Watson and the German soldier had to go their separate ways. 'Here, take this,' said Watson. It was a British coin – half a crown. The enemy soldier smiled at his new friend and gave him something in return. It was a German coin.

They never saw each other again.

The wound in Watson's arm needed urgent treatment. He was taken to a military hospital in Derby, near London. Once there he underwent an operation. First, the doctors put him to sleep using an anaesthetic.

When Watson awoke, his blurry eyes focused on something lying on his bedside cabinet. It was an ugly, jagged lump of metal sitting on a nice, clean bandage. Just then, a doctor appeared.

'Was that thing taken out of me?' asked Watson.

'Yes,' said the doctor. The lump was a piece of shrapnel from the bomb that had blasted Watson. Then the doctor added: 'Now we have a proposal to make to you.'

'What's that?' asked Watson.

'We would like to conduct an experiment on you, using a new medicine,' replied the doctor. 'Will you help us?'

'Of course I will help you.'

'Don't you want to hear what it entails first?'

'No, I'm sure it will be fine.'

'Well, the thing is, every soldier here before you has given it up.'

'I will not give it up.'

'Very well, then,' said the doctor finally. 'We would like you to allow yourself to be inoculated every hour, night and day, for several days.' Being inoculated meant getting an injection. 'You will get the needle in any part of the body you want – your arm, your bottom, anywhere.'

'Yes, I will do it on one condition,' said Watson. 'You see that piece of shrapnel there?' He pointed at the jagged object. 'I want to be able to show that to my grandchildren when they ask me "Grand-dad, what did you do in the war?" I want to be able to show them that and tell them the story. So can I have it?'

'Yes,' said the doctor. 'And we will give you more than that. You can have your X-Ray plate as well.' In those days, X-Ray photographs of wounds were recorded on glass plates.

After this conversation, the treatment began. Just as the doctor said, it lasted for several days. Watson was injected with purified water, which had been boiled and then cooled. The water contained the medicine – but the doctor didn't tell Watson what it was.

The days went by and Watson thought about his men on the battlefield. He remembered his last words: 'I'll be back in a minute.'

When the treatment was finished the doctor was pleased. 'You will be delighted to hear you have really exceeded what we wanted,' he said to Watson. 'You have been marvellous. So shall we tell you what the medicine is?'

'Yes please,' said Watson.

'Let me begin by telling you that had this been the First World War, then without any shadow of a doubt your arm would have had to be chopped off,' said the doctor gravely. 'That would have been the only way to save you from a killer infection. No question.'

Watson listened intently as the doctor continued.

'Because of this new medicine, your arm has been saved. And the name of the medicine is penicillin.'

Penicillin was a substance discovered in 1928 by a Scottish medical scientist called Alexander Fleming. During the Second World War, penicillin was turned into a medicine and given to people for the first time to see how effective it was. Doctors also wanted to check that it was safe.

Hundreds of Allied soldiers like Lance-Sergeant Watson were treated with this great Scottish discovery, and many lives were saved. Penicillin went on to be one of the most important medicines ever created.

Now Watson was back on his feet at last. Although he was still recuperating, he had the opportunity to taste a little freedom. So he spoke to a young nurse with whom he had become friendly.

'I'll take you out if you like,' he said.

'Go on then,' she replied.

With his arm in a sling, Watson went into Derby town with the off-duty nurse. They walked past a pub, and she said: 'Let's go into this pub for a drink.'

'I'm sorry,' said Watson. 'I don't drink. I never touch alcohol.'

The nurse was not happy, and that was the end of their friendship.

'That's just the way I am,' said Watson.

In fact, Lance-Sergeant Watson had a reputation for being a bit different. Back in Scotland near the start of the war, his company had been billeted for a while in a whisky distillery. The distillery was bombed by the Luftwaffe – the German Air Force – and whisky leaked out of the casks. The other men helped themselves to it, but Watson never touched alcohol.

Another fact that made Watson different was that he was an

atheist. Being an atheist meant that he did not have a religion, and did not believe in God. This view of things was not very popular in the army at the time. Watson was often in trouble with superiors who did not accept his atheism.

On the other hand, Watson did have very strong political beliefs. He believed in an ideology called socialism. This meant he believed very strongly that people should be treated equally and fairly.

Watson had fought in the war on the front line, but he also fought against unfairness wherever he found it. Unfairness and injustice were not just on the enemy side. They sometimes found it on the Allied side, too.

There were two examples of unfairness on his own side that really stuck in Watson's mind. Just like ugly bits of shrapnel.

When Watson was a Lance-Corporal at his barracks in Maryhill, he saw how Catholic soldiers in his own regiment were treated unfairly. On Sunday they were not permitted to go to church like the Protestant men, because no officer would accompany them.

Watson said: 'I will escort you Catholic men to your church.'

'Why are you doing this for us, sir?' the Catholic soldiers asked as they marched up the hill.

'I don't agree with your religious belief,' replied Watson. 'But I will defend to the death your right to believe it!'

Later on in the war, just before Watson fought in Normandy, he encountered another example of unfairness and injustice. This happened when he was seconded to a division of the United States Army, which was stationed in Britain. Being seconded meant being transferred temporarily to another force.

At first, being a Scottish soldier in the US Army was fun. In the British Army, Watson had been given just one egg a week in his food ration. In the US Army you got two eggs *every day*. What a feast!

Plus, Watson was treated like a bit of a celebrity. The American soldiers were very impressed by the formal way Watson saluted his superior officers. They all tried to copy his march and the way he loudly clicked his tackety boots when he held his hand up in a salute.

But the Americans could never get the hang of it. The rubber soles of their US Army boots were too soft, and their salutes were too casual.

Because Watson was an NCO, or Non-Commissioned Officer, he was assigned a driver to transport him from place to place. This was one of the perks of being in the US Army. Watson's driver was an African-American, and the two men got on very well.

One day, Watson's driver announced that he had some holidays coming up. 'I was thinking of going to Glasgow,' he said. 'I hear it is a good place to go on leave.'

'Yes, it certainly is,' Watson replied. 'Have you got anywhere to stay?'

'I was thinking I would book in somewhere,' said the driver cheerfully.

'Nonsense!' said Watson. 'You can stay with my mother. She would be delighted to have you. I'll give you the address.'

The driver's face fell. 'Oh no, I couldn't do that, Sir,' he said.

'Why on earth not?' said Watson, slightly offended.

'Look at me,' said the driver.

'I'm looking at you,' said Watson. 'What's the problem?'

'Look at me!' said the driver again.

'I *am* looking at you!' replied Watson. 'What's the problem?'

'I'm black, Sir!'

'What's that got to do with anything?' said Watson.

'Sir, if my superiors found out that a black man like me had spent the night alone in a white woman's house, I would be put up on a charge.' This meant the driver would be punished for misconduct.

'What!?' Watson had never heard anything so ridiculous.

This was the rule in the US Army, the driver explained. There was nothing that could be done. Black soldiers were second-class citizens and did not have the same freedom or rights as white soldiers. They were treated unfairly and unjustly.

Watson was outraged. The Allies were supposed to be fighting the German Army and their Nazi leaders because they treated people badly. The Allies were supposed to stand for democracy, which meant all were treated fairly and all had their freedom. Except, for many people, this was obviously not true.

'What is this so-called democracy we are fighting for!?' said Watson to his driver.

Watson ended his secondment with the US Army and bid his driver farewell. Watson often wondered what happened to him. After the war, black Americans fought and struggled at home for their freedom – but they would have to wait more than 20 years before they won it.

So there was a lot for Watson to reflect on while he completed his recovery from his wounds. He never saw any further combat, and was happy and relieved when the war finally ended in victory for the Allies over Nazi Germany in 1945.

Around this time Watson was discharged from active service and given a new job as an army instructor. He was also reunited with his girlfriend. The couple married and settled down in Glasgow to family life.

This was not quite the end of Lance-Sergeant Watson's wartime adventure. Something happened in the late 1940s, a few years after the war ended.

Watson was walking down the street in the town of Paisley, near Glasgow, when he felt a tap on his shoulder. He turned around and saw a face he recognised.

'That was a bloody long minute you took!' said the face. It was the soldier Watson had left in the dugout on the battlefield.

'Am I pleased to see you,' said Watson's old comrade. 'We all thought you were dead!'

'Aye,' said Watson with a smile. 'It was a long minute.'

WAR REPORT

Personnel: Stewart Watson. He was recruited in Glasgow, where he began his military career at Maryhill Barracks with the 13th Battalion Highland Light Infantry. He was made a Lance-Corporal and posted to Aberdeenshire for training and coastal defence duties in 1940–41. He was later seconded to the United States Army for a while.

In 1944 he was a Lance-Sergeant in the Glasgow Highlanders and fought in France after the D-Day landings. The D-Day landings were the beginning of a big push by the Allies against the German Army, which had taken control of Europe. Watson was wounded at the Battle for Caen in Normandy and returned home. He was discharged from active service in 1945 and reassigned as an army instructor.

Event log: The Battle for Caen. To pronounce Caen try saying it as 'Khan' but don't stress the letter 'n'. This battle was fought in June 1944. German Panzer tank divisions defended the town from Allied attack. The German firepower was so strong that the Allies were pinned down in cornfields outside the town and unable to advance. Among these Allies were Lance-Sergeant Watson and the Glasgow Highlanders.

The Allied commanders decided to try to encircle the town and close the net on the Germans. The fighting was very bloody and the battle raged for weeks. The town of Caen was reduced to rubble. Tens of thousands of civilians and soldiers were killed. Eventually, the Germans were forced to retreat. It was one of the most important Allied victories of the war.

Inventory: Penicillin. This medicine was discovered by Scottish medical scientist Alexander Fleming in his laboratory in London in 1928. Penicillin is a kind of friendly mould and Fleming observed that it could kill deadly bacteria. This made penicillin the world's first antibiotic.

Other scientists took Fleming's discovery and helped turn it into a usable drug. The first trial of penicillin as a medicine was carried out in 1941. Larger tests known as field trials were conducted on soldiers in 1943 and 1944. Among the subjects was Lance-Sergeant Watson. His wounded arm was saved from amputation and he made a full recovery.

CHAPTER 2

The Man with the Electric Gloves

Rear-gunner Willie Ritchie was flying through the night into the danger zone. Sitting in the cramped gun turret at the tail of a huge Wellington bomber, he peered through the turret's domed glass canopy.

He was scanning the dark sky for enemy fighters. He saw terrific flashes of light and puffs of smoke. The anti-aircraft guns on the ground 18,000 feet below him were on the attack.

Deadly bursts of flak exploded all around. The Wellington rattled and shook. Ritchie was rocked in his harness. He could smell the flak's explosive cordite. It smelled like nail varnish.

Ritchie and the rest of the Wellington's seven-man crew were on their first combat mission with the Royal Air Force, or RAF. The anti-aircraft guns were hard at work trying to make sure it would be their last.

Over the cockpit radio, the Bomb Aimer was giving instructions to the Pilot.

'Go right . . . Right . . . Steady . . . Steady . . .'

The Pilot adjusted the plane's course so that the Bomb Aimer would be right on target when he dropped his first payload – a photoflash bomb with the strength of 5,000 candles.

'Left a little . . . Bombs fused . . . Steady . . . Steady . . .'

Once the photoflash was released, a camera on the plane would automatically take pictures of enemy positions on the ground. These would be used by other planes to bomb the targets, and to help plan future operations.

At last came the magic words.

'Bombs gone!'

As the bomb fell, the Wellington had to hold a steady course so the camera could get clear pictures. The flak was intense. Ritchie could hear jagged bits of shrapnel ripping holes in the outer skin of the plane's wings and fuselage.

At last the run was completed. The Navigator gave the course for the Wellington's next target – the railway yards. The plane had taken off from RAF Peplow in England at 22.35 hours, or just after half-past ten at night. It was now after midnight.

The railway yards were quite near Paris. Ritchie and his crew had just flown over the coastline of Cherbourg, a corner of northwest France. Now they flew east towards the French capital.

The secondary target was in range at 01.15 hours. Again the Bomb Aimer, who lay flat on his stomach looking down, gave the Pilot instructions. Ritchie kept his eyes peeled for enemy fighters. His stomach churned with fear, which made him even more alert.

'Come on . . .' said Ritchie to himself, praying for the Bomb Aimer to give the signal that the second payload was away so they could head for home. Yet time seemed to stand still.

Eventually the magic words were heard again. 'Bombs gone!'

Ritchie looked down from his turret and saw the effects. Two separate items had been dropped. The first was a round of incendiary bombs, which were designed to start fires. These hit many buildings and set them ablaze. The second was propaganda leaflets, which were dropped to try to turn people on the ground against the enemy.

On the way back, the Wellington went for a second photo run over the Cherbourg coast. With just 20 minutes to go to the target zone, the enemy gave them a nasty surprise. Ritchie spotted it first. Coming in fast on the Wellington's port quarter – its left-hand side – was a Messerschmitt 110 fighter aircraft.

Ritchie radioed the Pilot. 'Prepare to corkscrew! My command word will be "Dive!"' he said. The Pilot acknowledged. The corkscrew was an emergency manoeuvre the Pilot would undertake to try to get the bomber out of trouble.

Ritchie opened fire on the Messerschmitt with his four .303 Browning machine guns. There was a deafening *rat-tat-tat-tat* sound as the bursts of ammunition were sprayed at the enemy aircraft.

Then Ritchie gave the order.

'Dive!'

Suddenly the Wellington plunged straight down, circling as it did so. It made a shape in the air just like a corkscrew. Inside the aircraft, anything that was not bolted down quickly fell out of place. There was a clatter as the Navigator's pencils, compasses and charts went everywhere.

The Wireless Operator under the windowed astrodome on top of the bomber reported that he could see smoke coming from the enemy fighter's engines, forcing it to make a hasty escape. The bomber levelled off and got back on course.

Luckily, Ritchie and his crewmates met no other fighters that night. They completed their second run over Cherbourg and then crossed the English Channel. They touched down back at base at 04.00 hours. Mission accomplished.

As the Wellington taxied off the runway and came to a stop, Ritchie undid his straps and removed his electric gloves. These special gloves were worn because of the freezing temperatures a gunner encountered at high altitude. The gloves had electric heat pads in them to keep his fingers warm so he could operate his guns.

It was funny to think that not so long ago, Ritchie's hands were kept warm in a very different way. They put loaves in and out of a bread oven.

When Britain declared war on Nazi Germany back in September 1939, Willie Ritchie had no idea he would one day be a bomber tail gunner. In those days he was a young apprentice baker. He learned how to bake loaves and pies in his home fishing village of Whitehills on the Aberdeenshire coast.

The young apprentice baker was also a keen footballer, and attended youth clubs at night. This was a way of meeting other lads – and pretty lassies. Eventually Ritchie found himself a girlfriend.

As far as Ritchie was concerned back then, the war sounded like a great big adventure. He listened with great excitement to early reports of the first air raids by RAF bomber aircraft on territory occupied by the German enemy. He longed for the day when he could take part in it all.

In February 1941, Ritchie took his first step on the road to fulfilling that dream. He joined his local Air Training Corps, or ATC. The ATC lads were drilled to follow orders, trained to keep themselves fit and given lessons in aircraft recognition.

Aircraft recognition was vital to anyone who would one day fly with the RAF. You had to be able to spot whether an approaching aircraft was friend or foe within seconds. Your life could depend on it.

Ritchie was keen and showed promise as a cadet. Eventually, he was selected to attend a week's training at RAF Lossiemouth on the Moray Firth coast, northeast of Inverness. Ritchie and the other lads were shown around the base to learn how things worked. They visited the control tower, the engine repair hangars, and the units where aircraft parachutes and dinghies were packed.

The highlight came on the Wednesday. Ritchie was picked first to climb into the open-air cockpit of a De Havilland Tiger Moth aeroplane. The Tiger Moth was a biplane, meaning it had two wings, one on top of the other. It would be Ritchie's first flight.

'Would you like me to perform a loop-the-loop?' asked the pilot once Ritchie was safely strapped in.

Ritchie gave the pilot a 'thumbs up' and away they went. The plane took off and, for the first time, Ritchie was airborne. He could see Lossiemouth and the Moray Firth below. Then the pilot did the loop-the-loop. When Ritchie put two thumbs up to show how much he enjoyed it, the pilot thought the young cadet meant 'Do it again!' and so he performed the manoeuvre for a second time.

On Friday Ritchie and the other cadets got their first chance to fly in the pride of RAF Lossiemouth – the Vickers Wellington bomber. This large aircraft required a six-man crew. While the pilot practised his take-offs and landings – known as circuits and bumps – Ritchie and the others tried out different jobs on board.

It was in the rear gun turret that Ritchie felt most at home. He used the controls to rotate the turret fully from side to side, or 'beam to beam'. He handled the guns and pointed them up and down.

At the end of the week Ritchie was invited for a chat with the Station Commander.

'Do you know what you would like to do in the RAF?' asked the Commander.

'Yes, sir,' replied Ritchie. 'I would like to be a rear gunner.'

'Very good,' said the Commander. 'You are the proper size for the turret.' Ritchie had a slim and compact body, which made him ideal for that position.

'But this is the most unenviable position in a bomber,' the Commander added.

Ritchie wondered why this was so.

'It carries quite a high incidence of death,' said the Commander gravely.

Knowing that rear gunner was the most dangerous position in the aircraft did not put Ritchie off. He still thought war was a great big adventure. As soon as he was old enough, Ritchie volunteered to join the air crew.

The RAF medical tests and entrance exams were held in Edinburgh. On the way there, Ritchie threw pennies out of the window of the steam train as it passed over the Forth Bridge. He made a wish that he would pass the tests.

As luck would have it – or maybe it was just down to his talent and hard work – he passed with flying colours. Ritchie was now a fully fledged RAF Aircrew cadet.

Ritchie received orders to report to Lord's Cricket Ground, at St John's Wood, in London. There he would begin his training. Before that, he was allowed ten days at home.

On the platform at Aberdeen Station, Ritchie looked very smart and suddenly more grown up in his ATC uniform. His mother and girlfriend were there to bid him farewell. This was the beginning of his great big war adventure. Everyone had mixed feelings about it. They were excited and nervous. Ritchie hugged and kissed his loved ones and then boarded the train to London.

'Goodbye then,' he said. The train shunted away from the platform in a cloud of smoke and steam, and headed south.

The carriage was packed with war servicemen and service-women, but Ritchie was in his own private thoughts. How will I get on with the other cadets? Will I be able to cope with what lies ahead?

After many hours the train ground to a halt on the outskirts of London, where it waited for a while. Suddenly some dramatic events unfolded in the distance. The windows of the carriage became like a huge cinema screen, as Ritchie and the others looked at the scene.

Huge beams of light from searchlights swept across the sky. The enemy was bombing London from the skies. Anti-aircraft 'Ack-Ack' guns on the ground fired explosive shells into the air to try to damage enemy aircraft. This was the infamous London Blitz, a series of night-time attacks by the German Air Force that seemed never to end.

'I can see a German bomber going down in flames!' shouted

one soldier. At that moment, Ritchie knew that if his training was successful, he would soon be getting the same treatment as that bomber from enemy guns on the ground in France and Germany.

At last the train pulled into King's Cross Station. As Ritchie stepped on to the platform, he realised he had no idea how to get to St John's Wood from there. He bumped into another cadet who was also a bit lost.

Luckily, at the entrance to the station, they buttonholed a third lad in ATC uniform who knew the way. The three young cadets took the underground train. When they climbed the steps back up to street level, they found themselves among twenty or so other raw recruits.

The group were met by a gruff RAF Sergeant. He began barking orders at them right away, and marched them to Lord's Cricket Ground to begin the training.

Lord's Cricket Ground was the home of a famous cricket club, but for now it had been converted into a wartime RAF training camp. Ritchie had several important things to do to get started.

First, he had to make a will in case he was killed in action. This meant writing down what he wanted to be done with his things when he died. The only possession he had was his bike, so this didn't take long.

Next, he had to go up a broad staircase to a long room with windows overlooking the cricket pitches. This was where the cadets were given a medical check-up to make sure they were fit for duty.

The cadets were lined up in two rows alongside each other and asked to take off their clothes. Since they were all shy young lads, they hesitated about doing this.

'Strip!' shouted the gruff Sergeant angrily. 'He seems to enjoy bullying us,' Ritchie thought to himself.

The cadets promptly took off all their clothes. Then a doctor in a white coat, holding a torch, inspected their bodies. After it was done, Ritchie and the others had to pick their clothes up in a bundle under their right arm. They picked up their suitcases with their left hand, and then turned right.

'Oh dear,' thought Ritchie to himself as he looked at what was coming next. The naked men were now standing in two queues facing female nurses from the Women's Auxiliary Air Force, known as the WAAF. The WAAF nurses were handing syringes to male doctors. The cadets were each given several injections to protect them against any diseases or serious illnesses they might pick up while on duty.

The embarrassment of standing naked in front of the ladies was soon forgotten. The cocktail of injections was overpowering and Ritchie felt drowsy. Many of the lads slumped to the floor. After a while, they recovered and got dressed again.

Just before lunch, Ritchie was shown his billet. A billet was a bed for the night. Although the rooms were cramped, with seven men in each, at least it would be somewhere to rest.

Lunch was greedily wolfed down. Then the cadets were taken to the clothing store to be kitted out. This was a highlight of the day. The cadets got a dress uniform for such occasions as formal parades. They also got their battle dress, which was a uniform for wearing on active duty. RAF uniforms were very well made, and lots of measurements were taken to ensure that Ritchie's fitted him perfectly.

Finally, Ritchie was given his own mug, knife, fork and two spoons. He also got shoe brushes and a shaving brush. It was up to him to look after all these things and not lose them.

Ritchie's eyes were tested carefully by an optician to make sure he had perfect vision. This was an essential quality for a gunner if he was to aim his guns accurately.

For four weeks, the cadets were trained hard. Ritchie learned everything, from the rules of flying to the procedure for using a parachute if he had to jump out of the aircraft during an emergency. There was lots of physical fitness training. Ritchie made a couple of good new friends along the way. On Saturdays the lads were permitted to explore London using a free Armed Forces' ticket for the buses, trains and underground.

Even training could be a bumpy ride at times, though. Ritchie and his closest pal during training, who was called John, fell foul of the gruff Sergeant a few times. The Sergeant seemed to find any excuse to put the pair on 'jankers'. This was a bit like getting a detention or punishment at school, but worse. Ritchie and his mate had to wash dishes, peel potatoes and chop firewood.

It was obvious the Sergeant was a bully, so Ritchie decided to get his own back. He filled the sugar container up with salt, and the salt one with sugar, while he was on jankers in the Sergeants' Mess. The Mess was a place where officers could eat their meals and relax. They were not very relaxed when they ended up with sugary potatoes and salty custard! The gruff Sergeant was blamed and he never bothered Ritchie again.

When the four weeks at St John's Wood were up, Ritchie was moved to different places around the country, including Bridlington on England's east coast and the Isle of Man to the west.

He was taught how to handle the tool of his trade – the .303 Browning machine gun. After a week of intensive practice, Ritchie could take the gun apart and put it back together again blindfolded. The blindfold was used because there would be no light on board an operational bomber. Ritchie would have to be able to operate his guns, and fix them if necessary, in total darkness.

The gunners practised shooting using real guns, but they also used simulators that were a bit like the WW2 shoot-em-up computer games we might play today. In Ritchie's day there were no personal computers or games consoles. Instead, the simulators used a more simple technology of film projectors, but they were very realistic. Clouds and enemy aircraft were projected on to a huge white bowl. The trainee gunner sat facing this bowl and targeted the enemy aircraft in his sights. Ritchie's score was recorded.

On the Isle of Man, Ritchie took to the skies in real aircraft. These training bombers were called Avro Ansons, with a crew of five. Ritchie found that the RAF armourers deliberately put faults in his guns to see how he coped. He had to use his training to fix any problems, and then let rip on the targets. Again his score was counted.

Often, the gunners practised with cine-cameras instead of guns in case they damaged the practice aircraft. Again, using these cameras was a bit like playing a computer game. Except with the din of the aircraft engines and the wind whistling through the cabin, it was all very real.

Besides this practical training, there were other important tests. Ritchie and the cadets had to be able to read and write well to complete these tests successfully. They had to do oral exams, too, which meant being able to speak well, and answer questions clearly and sensibly.

It was now January 1943 and there were only a few weeks to

go before Ritchie was expected to be ready for his first combat mission. Every day he was reminded of the dangers he faced, and not just from the enemy. He and the others had a long, freezing dip in the sea when they were ordered to jump into a harbour and retrieve a dinghy that was turned upside down and put it the right way up again. The dinghy could be a real life-saver if a plane crash-landed in water – but if a rough sea capsized the dinghy and you couldn't put it right, you would be doomed.

After 17 weeks in the RAF, Ritchie faced his moment of truth. The pass list of all the cadets who had completed the training successfully was put up. He asked himself nervously: 'Is my name going to be on it?'

It was.

At 10 o'clock the next morning, Ritchie and the other successful cadets were paraded before their Commanding Officer. A military band struck up a tune and Ritchie went up to the dais, which is a platform used for public ceremonies. The Commanding Officer gave him his Sergeant's stripes and – best of all – his Gunner's Wings. These would be put on his uniform to show that Willie Ritchie was now a Sergeant Air Gunner in the RAF.

There were now a couple of weeks' home leave before Ritchie would join his Operational Training Unit. He said goodbye to John, who had been a constant friend during training. They hoped they would be posted to the same airbase on their return. Sadly, Ritchie never saw his friend again. Ritchie got orders to go to RAF Peplow, in Shropshire, which is in western England. John was sent to a different base and on his second combat operation over France, he was shot down and killed.

When Ritchie arrived at RAF Peplow after another emotional

farewell to his family, he was pleased to see that there was at least one friendly face. Don Perry was a Welshman whom Ritchie had first met on the platform at King's Cross Station, when they had arrived to begin their training months ago. Back then they had been boys. Now they felt like men, and ready for action. Ritchie and Perry vowed to try to make sure they were in the same crew.

A total of 105 crewmen were given a cup of tea and instructed to get to know each other. There were fifteen each of the following types of crewmen – Pilots, Navigators, Wireless Operators (W.Ops.), Bomb Aimers, Flight Engineers, and a total of 28 Gunners. Divide the total of 105 by seven and what did you have?

Answer: 15 bomber crews, made up of seven men each – and each with his own crucial job to do.

'Over the next few days you will all have to get to know each other,' said the Commander. 'After five days, you must then arrange yourselves into crews with men that you feel happy with.'

'Oh, and one other thing . . .' he added. The men all listened. 'You must not wash or shave until further notice.'

Whiskers slowly grew on Ritchie's chin while he spent the next five days racking up many hours of flight training aboard a Wellington bomber. The crew also had to attend lectures on what each other's jobs were – just in case a Gunner suddenly had to try his hand at being a Bomb Aimer in an emergency.

On the fifth day, it became clear why the men had been told not to wash or shave. They were dressed in civilian clothes and photographed. They had to carry copies of their passport-sized picture on them in case they landed behind enemy lines.

The idea was that an area's local Resistance movement, who

helped the Allies against Nazi Germany, would make false passes using these photographs. The RAF airmen could then slip through the enemy checkpoints dressed as civilians, and escape.

So the men in the pictures needed to look dirty and dishevelled in order to pass as harassed civilians during wartime. Plus they would be more likely to look like that anyway after a week or two spent hiding in enemy territory!

At last, a hot shower and a shave. Then all 105 men met once more in the crew room. It was now time for Ritchie to get 'married'. This meant he now had to marry into a crew. Ritchie and Perry had already agreed to fly together. Eventually the seven-man crew was assembled as follows:

Pilot: Bob Cairns, from Edinburgh, Scotland. His job was to fly the aircraft.

Flight Engineer: Eynon Rees, from Cardiff, Wales. He would assist the Pilot with the flaps and landing gear, and look after the engine supplies. Plus if the Bomb Aimer was injured, he would have to take over.

Navigator: Reg Cann, from Bath, England. His job would be to give the Pilot the information needed to get the aircraft to the correct target and back, and in the correct time.

Wireless Operator (W.Op.): Percy Ansell, from Essex, England. He would be in charge of communications and operate the wireless radio. He would assist the Navigator, especially with weather reports. He also would man the astrodome at the top of the aircraft to keep an eye out for enemy fighters.

Bomb Aimer: John Crew, from Oshawa, Canada. Responsible for the bomb load, as well as cameras and photo flares. If the plane came under fighter attack, he would have to man the front gun turret.

Mid-Upper Gunner: Don Perry, from Wales. Required to keep his eyes peeled at all times and stay cool under pressure. Must instantly recognize when an enemy fighter is approaching and warn the Pilot. He would also have to be a sharpshooter.

Rear Gunner: Willie Ritchie, from Whitehills, Scotland. Duties very similar to the Mid-Upper Gunner. Ritchie's would be the coldest and loneliest post on the aircraft. It would be the hottest when under attack, because the Rear Gunner is a prime target for enemy fighters.

This crew bonded together very strongly and, over time, those who flew under Pilot Bob Cairns would become known in the service as 'Cairns' Bairns'. Of the 15 crews assembled at RAF Peplow at that moment, Cairns' Bairns would be the only crew to survive the war.

On his 92nd day of operational training, Ritchie saw his name and that of his crew on the Battle Order for the very first time. He felt a shiver down his spine. 'This is it,' he thought to himself. 'Tonight I will face the enemy in combat.'

16.40 hours, or just after half-past four. The crew did their checks on the Wellington bomber. Ritchie had to check that everything in his gun turret was working.

Hydraulics and electrics powering the turret and guns: *check*.

Ammunition and belts carrying ammunition to the turret: *check*

Machine gun alignment and gun reflector sight: *check*.

Dead Man's Lever, used to pull the gunner out of the turret if he is injured: *check*.

Oxygen lines and spare oxygen bottle for survival at high altitude: *check*.

19.00 hours. First operational briefing. The seven crews sat in rows in the briefing room, gazing at a curtained wall in front of them. Ritchie and the others stood to attention as the Wing Commander and his briefing team trooped into the room. The doors were locked and guards posted outside. It was all Top Secret.

The Commander greeted the men and welcomed them to their first operational briefing. Then the curtain was drawn back. On the wall was a map of Europe, with targets indicated by red and green ribbons. The red ribbons were targets to be hit on the outward leg of the journey; the green ribbons were targets to hit on the way back home.

'Timing will be essential,' said the Navigation Leader, as he went over the routes each bomber was to take.

'You must find the exact aiming point,' said the Bombing Leader, as he explained what bombs were to be dropped and where.

'These are the types of enemy fighters you will probably encounter,' said the Gunnery Leader, who discussed the fighters and pointed out where the Ack-Ack anti-aircraft guns were.

'If you are taken prisoner, only reveal your name and number. Nothing else,' warned the Intelligence Officer.

Finally, there was a brief weather report by a man from the Met Office and a last word from the Commander, who wished them all the best on their first meeting with the enemy.

20.20 hours. The crews were sent for a shower and a change

of underclothing. As a gunner, Ritchie had to wear long silk underpants and a silk vest to help protect him from the extreme cold weather when the plane was flying at a great height. The temperature in Ritchie's gun turret could drop as low as –40°C.

20.45 hours. The operational meal. This dinner was very special. A last chance for a bit of relaxed banter. Everyone knew that if a crew were unlucky, it would be their last supper. After dinner, the men were sent to the locker rooms to empty their pockets of anything that could help the Germans if they were captured and interrogated. Letters, bus tickets, cinema ticket stubs, receipts – you name it. They were allowed photographs of girlfriends or wives, provided no information was written on them.

On his way to the aircraft, Ritchie collected a number of important items:

Parachute. In an emergency, he would rotate his turret all the way round and fall out of the canopy backwards. After falling free of the aircraft, he would open his chute and hope for the best.

Electric flight clothes. Electrically heated overalls, socks and gloves, designed to offer protection from the cold.

A .38 revolver. In case of landing behind enemy lines, he needed to defend himself.

Evasion pack. To help him survive if he landed in dangerous country. The pack contained malted milk tablets and sweets, water-purifying tablets, Benzedrine tablets to keep him awake in an emergency, and morphine to kill pain if he was wounded. There were also matches, needles and thread, a fishing line, a razor and soap, and a compass.

More tiny compasses were hidden in his battledress buttons, and in his shoe heels he had lighters for starting fires. The most important survival item was a map of Europe, which was made of silk. This made it light and easy to fold and, unlike a paper one, it wouldn't get ruined if it got wet.

A small bus driven by a WAAF took Ritchie and his crewmates to their waiting Wellington bomber. The driver was a young woman and she had tears in her eyes as she wished Ritchie and the others good luck. She had taken rookie crews out before who never returned.

The last stage before take-off was to conduct pre-flight checks and have a chat and cup of tea with the Ground Crew. The RAF Ground Crew were the unsung heroes of the war. Working on planes for long hours and often in freezing conditions, they faced extreme hazards from propeller blades that would take a man's head off if he lost concentration. If the Ground Crew did not keep the planes in working order, the flight crews would get nowhere.

22.00 hours. Ritchie and his crewmates boarded the aircraft for take-off, but not before first sharing out their flying rations – chocolate, sweets and chewing gum.

Ritchie climbed into his lonely gun turret, the only position in the plane that was cut off from the other crew. He put the hands in his electric gloves together and prayed for a successful mission. He prayed for his loved ones at home. The fear and dread of what was to come lay uppermost in his thoughts.

22.05 hours. Engines start. Slowly the plane taxied to the end of the runway, where the crew waited for the green light. It was a long wait and Ritchie's stomach was churning.

22.35 hours. Take off! Pilot Cairns made a great take-off and at last the crew were off into the unknown, to face the enemy for the first time.

This was the beginning of the mission to Cherbourg and then

the railway yards, and it ended in success. Further training followed aboard a four-engined Halifax bomber. Then came the big moment the entire crew had been waiting for. It was time to join the big boys. It was time to convert to the finest bomber in the world – the Lancaster.

The crew moved to RAF Hemswell to undergo a conversion course. They were then posted to their first heavy bomber squadron, 625 Kelstern. They were put on the Battle Order for their first mission in the squadron and assigned a Lancaster called 'V for Victor'.

The target was the German city of Kiel, in particular its harbour and yards containing U-Boat submarines. A total of 629 aircraft were dispatched on the mission. Ritchie's bomber was given a bomb load of 16,000 pounds of high explosives. Ritchie and his crew dropped their bombs and managed to evade the flak and enemy fighters. Others were not so lucky. Four Lancasters were shot down.

Several further missions followed. They attacked a flying-bomb launch site. They bombed industrial centres. They attacked railway lines and bridges. They attacked the German army. They bombed airfields during daylight to destroy German fighters before they had a chance to come out at night. They bombed the cities of Bremen, Stuttgart and others.

The success of these early bombing raids was noted by the RAF top brass. This led to the greatest moment of Ritchie's life. He and his crew were invited to join the Pathfinders of 8 Group.

The Pathfinder crews were the elite. Trained to arrive at targets before the main force of bombers, they identified aiming points and marked them with special coloured indicators. This allowed the rest of the bombers to see the targets clearly. Ritchie and his crew were posted to 582 Pathfinder Squadron in Little Staughton, which would remain their home until the end of the war.

As Pathfinders, Ritchie and his crewmates required two navigators to make sure they were accurate. So the crew increased from seven to eight. John Crew, the Bomb Aimer, became second Navigator. An Australian called Bob Curran became the new Bomb Aimer.

Hurricane and Thunderclap were the names given to major bombing operations that Ritchie and his crew took part in during 1944 and the beginning of 1945. German cities took a massive pounding on these raids, which were crucial in turning the war in favour of the Allies.

Losses among air crews were heavy. Sometimes things went disastrously wrong. On one mission that took place just before Christmas in 1944, the omens were bad from the start. Thick fog shrouded the runways and there were endless delays before the crews could take to the skies. When they eventually did, two Lancasters collided in mid-air because of the fog and sixteen men were killed.

The crews that continued with the mission soon got into hot water. The target area was the city of Cologne, but the cloud cover ended just before the bombers got there. The anti-aircraft fire was intense. All the bombers scored direct hits, but the lead Lancaster lost two engines and caught fire. It went into a spin and crashed to the ground, with only the Rear Gunner bailing out. He seemed destined for certain death, too, thought Ritchie as he watched his fellow gunner float down into the flaming city below. Amazingly, as it later turned out, he survived.

On the way back to base Ritchie and his Lancaster, called 'Z for Zebra', were attacked by a swarm of Messerschmitt 109s and Focke-Wulf 190s. Three Lancasters were shot down returning home over Belgium. Ritchie and the rest of his crew made it back in one piece in time for Christmas dinner and seven days' leave.

In February 1945, Ritchie and his crew took part in Operation Thunderclap. This operation was intended to try to crush Germany, which was now really struggling against the Allies. The RAF would bomb such cities as Berlin, Chemnitz, Dresden and Leipzig in order to assist the Russian Red Army who were attacking Germany from the east.

The main target on the night of 13 February was the beautiful, historic city of Dresden. This city was attacked by hundreds of aircraft dropping thousands of tonnes of bombs. It was already a blazing inferno when Bob Cairns, Ritchie's Pilot, began his bombing run. As the plane circled the target, Ritchie could see a fire-storm caused by the bombs sweeping across the city. It destroyed everything in its path. Historians believe that around 25,000 people in the city were killed by the bombs, and hundreds of thousands were badly injured.

Ritchie continued to take part in operations, night and day, bombing towns and cities large and small. RAF losses continued to mount and the number of Rear Gunners dwindled. Ritchie found himself being asked to help out other crews when his own crew were not in action. On one such occasion Ritchie was part of the crew of the Master Bomber aircraft which led almost 600 Lancasters on a bombing raid on the city of Kiel. A German battleship was sunk and two others severely damaged. Three shipyards and a U-Boat yard were damaged. On these and other bombing raids, many tens of thousands of men, women and children were killed.

On 8 May 1945, Germany finally surrendered. The bombing runs of Ritchie and his comrades had helped defeat the enemy. But it was not time to breathe a sigh of relief just yet. The war in Europe was not quite over. There was still work to be done.

Families across the continent were starving. The war had destroyed farms, food factories and shops. People were desperate, and would die of starvation if urgent help was not provided. An operation was set up called Manna. This meant that the RAF bombers would convert to dropping food parcels instead of bombs. The name Manna comes from a story in the Bible. It is the word for the food handed down to the Israelites by God when they were starving in the wilderness.

Ritchie's plane flew in low – no higher than 500 feet, or 150 metres, above ground. The country beneath them was Holland, and the Dutch people waved flags from rooftops and church spires. There were some German soldiers who stood by, defeated. Some of them decided to have a pot-shot at the Lancaster with their rifles because it was flying so low, but they could not inflict much damage.

The food parcels were dropped. Sweets, teddy bears and books that WAAFs and airmen had given the crew were dropped for the children. Ritchie saw people desperately scrabbling to get their hands on as many of the packages as they could carry.

Years later Ritchie met a Dutch man selling flower bulbs in Aberdeenshire. That man had once been a boy whose life was saved by a food parcel. 'You are one of the Manna boys!' said the man joyfully, and gave Ritchie a hug. 'When the food parcels fell and some of them burst open in the forest, we children licked the butter from the trees. We were so hungry! Thanks and thanks again.'

Back in 1945, it had been a comfort to Ritchie know that the Manna operation was doing some good. 'For once we are helping, not killing or destroying,' thought Ritchie to himself at the time, and later wrote this in his war diary.

When the smoke of battle cleared, the utter devastation inflicted on villages, towns and cities across Europe became very clear. In the summer of 1945, Ritchie and his crew continued to fly across the continent, bringing weary Allied troops back home and gathering up prisoners of war.

On Saturday, 4 August 1945, Ritchie and the rest of Cairns' Bairns took off from a place called Bari in southern Italy with 20 exhausted but relieved soldiers on board. The men were 'demob happy' – delighted that war was over and eager to have some fun. After seven hours and 20 minutes the aircraft landed and came to a halt. The engines and propellers came to a stop and Ritchie quietly looked around his gun turret for the last time. He would never fly again.

The crew said their goodbyes to each other at a farewell meal. They shared stories. Some of them were happy and funny, some sad and depressing. Percy Ansell, the Wireless Operator, recalled how many times he had looked down through the night sky at the gigantic smoking inferno of yellow and orange flame, caused when hundreds of Lancasters bombed a town or city such as Cologne or Dresden. 'It was like looking into Hell,' said Ansell, and they all agreed.

War was not the adventure that Ritchie had been expecting when he was a young apprentice baker. It was a much bigger, more dreadful, more terrifying and more exciting adventure than he had ever imagined.

The war was over, but the memories remained. The experience had turned Ritchie from a boy into a man. He married and started a family, settling in Whitehills. He realised a baker's life was not for him, and instead he became a nurse. It was a job he really loved. He also kept in touch, on and off, with his old flying comrades.

After many decades, a reunion of the Cairns' Bairns Lancaster crew was arranged. A few years after that Ritchie, by then an elderly man, was a special guest at an airshow and got to sit in the rear gun turret of a Lancaster once again.

These were happy experiences that reminded Ritchie of all the good things about the war: the camaraderie of friends pulling together and working hard in a tough situation; the excitement of flying; the satisfaction of doing a job to the best of your abilities; the realization that you have triumphed over an enemy that was in the wrong, and needed to be defeated, to bring more peace and happiness to the world.

Then there were the bad things about war, things that had to be questioned. Why must we fight each other? What does war do to our hearts? When does an act of war go too far, and become a crime?

Ritchie thought about these things when he decided to visit Cologne cathedral, almost 50 years after he and his fellow RAF bombers had wreaked devastation on that city during the final acts of the war. The city was rebuilt after that, and new generations had made it a peaceful and prosperous place once again. But they never forgot what happened there between 1943 and 1945.

The huge cathedral, known to locals as the Kölner Dom, had been damaged quite badly by the Lancaster bombers. People said it was a miracle it never collapsed. After the war, it was repaired and restored.

At the entrance, Ritchie saw a message written on the wall. It said that the RAF bombers were murderers.

That *he* was a murderer.

He walked in.

The huge cavern of the old stone cathedral echoed with the quiet chatter of hundreds of visitors. Tourists filled the place; lighting candles, reading guidebooks and taking pictures. Many of them were young people born decades after the war ended.

They hardly noticed the small elderly Scottish man who had sat down on a pew by himself, and become lost in his own private thoughts. His hands were gently clasped together in quiet prayer.

'I pray for my family,' he whispered.

'I pray for the friends I lost while bombing this city,' he added.

'I pray for the many citizens who lost their lives,' he said.

He looked up at all the people milling about the cathedral.

'I feel so alone,' he thought. Then he got up from the pew, and left.

WAR REPORT

Personnel: Willie Ritchie. As a teenager, in 1941, he joined his local Air Training Corps in Aberdeenshire. He passed his RAF entrance exams in Edinburgh. His training was based at St John's Wood in London and other locations. He graduated as a Sergeant Air Gunner. He flew his first combat operations in Wellington bombers before converting to a Lancaster bomber. In late 1944 he joined the elite 582 Pathfinder Squadron based at RAF Little Staughton, and became a Warrant Officer.

Ritchie and his crew became known as Cairns' Bairns after their Pilot, Bob Cairns. Ritchie flew dozens of heavy bombing missions over occupied Europe, sometimes as a Master Bomber crewman. At the end of the war in 1945 he flew several humanitarian missions, giving Manna food aid. He was awarded the Distinguished Flying Medal, or DFM, among other honours, for his exemplary service.

Event log: Operation Thunderclap, February 1945. One of many major RAF bombing operations Ritchie and his crew took part in. Thunderclap was intended to help bring the Second World War to a quick end. Among the cities bombed by the Lancaster crews were the German capital of Berlin, along with Chemnitz, Essen and Leipzig. Some places, such as the historic city of Dresden, were almost completely destroyed. Many tens of thousands of civilians were killed during these bombing raids.

Inventory: Avro Lancaster heavy bomber. Powered by four supercharged Rolls Royce Merlin piston engines. The RAF's most successful Second-World-War bomber aircraft. It usually had a crew of seven inside its metal fuselage. The Pathfinder squadrons had a crew of eight. The Lancaster was defended by eight machine guns, and could carry gigantic 'earthquake' bombs weighing up to 10,000kg.

CHAPTER 3

Drive and Determination

Noise was ringing in Anne Meldrum's ears as she took one hand off the huge steering wheel to drop down a gear. The engine and transmission grunted, whined and roared. It was as though the hulking Red Cross military ambulance were locked in battle with the monstrous winter gale outside. The storm rocked the vehicle on its chassis and blasted snow against the windscreen, but still the truck trundled on.

To add to the din, the windscreen wipers chattered incessantly as they flapped back and forth. Not that they helped much. Each sweep cleared the white film off the screen only long enough for Meldrum to see yet more white – an endless sea of white, with hardly anything to distinguish the sky from the road and surrounding fields except for the narrow pathways dug out of the snow.

Meldrum had to thread the ambulance through the steep banks of snow on either side of the path. At one moment she quickly fed the steering wheel through her hands to swerve around a nasty pothole – only for the axles to jolt violently over an icy ridge. 'Steady!' shouted a voice from the back, 'He won't take another bump like that!'

It was Lydia, Meldrum's colleague and best friend. The two young women were Red Cross nurses. Their task was to transport a seriously ill patient from the town of Keith to a hospital in Aberdeen, a distance of fifty miles. Ordinarily, the journey would have been routine. But the winter of 1942 was no ordinary winter. It was as severe as anyone could remember. The war now wasn't just against Nazi Germany – it was against the elements, too.

In the back of the ambulance with Lydia lay the patient – a man with bleeding lungs. Every crack in the road seemed to bring him closer to death's door. And yet there could be no let-up in the pace of the journey. If he didn't get to the hospital soon, he would surely die.

They were driving through the Glens of Foudland, a desolate and rugged hilly region of northeast Scotland. The nurses had picked up their patient at the small local hospital in Keith, which lacked the facilities needed to treat him. Despite the urgency of the situation, the Ward Sister had not been very happy to see them.

'Which one of you is the nurse?' the Sister had asked, glowering at them.

Meldrum and her friend looked at each other. 'Well . . .' said Meldrum hesitantly, 'we are both Red Cross nurses.'

'So you are not properly trained nurses, then? Hmmph!' said the Sister. She was very cross. 'This is ridiculous!' she barked. 'The patient is haemorrhaging from the lungs and has to be taken to Aberdeen. He requires expert medical attention!'

The shortages caused by the war meant there were no fully trained nurses available. This did not mean the Red Cross military nurses were complete amateurs. They had been trained in first aid, such as supporting broken bones with a wooden splint, and bandaging. Plus they knew how to administer injections. In fact Meldrum and her friend often helped a travelling doctor to give medical demonstrations in front of people, with one nurse acting as his assistant and the other pretending to be the patient. But this time, the situation was real.

'We'll do our very best,' Meldrum reassured the Sister. As Meldrum put the ambulance in gear and released the handbrake, she tried to console herself with the knowledge that at this moment the health of the vehicle under her command was of the utmost importance if the patient was to be saved. And when it came to servicing the ambulance – whether checking and refilling the oil or cleaning the spark plugs – Meldrum was on top of her game.

She was one of the very few women in the northeast of Scotland to have held a driving licence before the war. This was one of the reasons why she had been selected to become a driver. She had passed a special second test to drive the ambulance, and now had to use all of her skills to get the vehicle and its fragile cargo safely to Aberdeen.

Eventually, after a long and frightening slog through the snowy hills, the ambulance reached its destination. 'I've never been more thankful to see a journey over,' whispered Meldrum to herself as she killed the engine. Then she and Lydia took the patient out by the stretcher and into the hospital.

Meldrum looked at the face of the poor soul on the stretcher, hoping that the treatment he was about to receive would save

SCOTTISH TALES OF ADVENTURE

him. Seeing him lying there, she wondered what had become of her husband, Jack. He was away fighting on the front line in faraway lands. Was he safe and well? Or lying injured somewhere?

They had only been married a few weeks before he was sent off to fight in Burma, a place where the war was said to be very grim and the fighting very bloody. He had been given no leave to return home. Weeks apart from each other had stretched into months, and now years. She wondered, would she ever see him again?

To keep herself going while her husband was away Meldrum realised there was nothing for it but to roll up her sleeves up and do her bit on the Home Front. This meant her work as a Red Cross nurse, but there were other duties too. She and Lydia ran the local Young Men's Christian Association (YMCA) canteen in their home town of Banff.

'Scrambled eggs!' shouted Lydia to the young soldiers, who were seated around the canteen playing cards and chatting under clouds of cigarette smoke. It was a typical evening in the Banff YMCA canteen.

On the spinning turntable of the record player was a disc of American Big Band jazz music. The swinging sound of saxophone, double bass and drums beaten gently with brushes wafted out of the crackling loudspeaker.

'It's no that powdered egg stuff again, is it Lydia?' asked one of the smiling soldiers in a broad Glasgow accent, as the men shuffled past the counter and picked up the plates of powdered eggs, toast and mugs of steaming hot tea.

'Until Prime Minister Churchill decides to do away with

wartime rations,' Meldrum cut in, 'it will be powdered eggs for you for a good long while, young man!' She smiled at Lydia. They both burst out laughing.

'I hear you can get real eggs from local farmers if you play your cards right,' said the soldier who was next up – a tall, handsome young man with a sing-song foreign accent. He was Norwegian.

Lydia looked at the Norwegian and smiled. 'Perhaps for you they might make an exception,' she said.

The Norwegian held her gaze and smiled back at her. Lydia blushed.

'You know, Lydia's mother likes meeting new people and learning about things,' said Meldrum aloud. 'Perhaps she might be interested in learning a bit of Norwegian, eh Lydia? After all, it is our duty to invite these young men, who are so far from home, into our parents' houses for a couple of hours in front of the fire on a cold evening, is it not?' She winked at the Norwegian, who was standing with his plate in one hand and mug in the other, trying not to look embarrassed.

'Stop it!' said Lydia, whose face had also gone bright red. 'Perhaps . . . yes . . . maybe, I'll see whether you might be accommodated sometime,' her voice addressed the soldier, but her eyes were fixed on the floor. He bowed ever so slightly while mumbling a quiet 'Thank you', then went and sat down.

Next in line was a Lance-Corporal from a Scottish regiment. He picked up his dinner and said to Meldrum, 'Please pass on our thanks again to your mother for letting us run amok in her dining room.'

Lydia shot her friend an enquiring glance.

'Oh, the great ping-pong tournament!' said Meldrum, laughing. It had become a regular fixture at her mother's house for some of the soldiers to use the dining room for table tennis, or ping-pong. 'So long as the table is polished afterwards, she is always very happy to accommodate you,' she said.

'We left that table so clean you could eat your dinner off it,' said the Lance-Corporal. Everyone laughed. Then he turned serious for a moment, and added: 'Still no sign of your husband getting a home leave, then?'

'No, it doesn't seem so,' said Meldrum, as she poured out more cups of tea from the stainless-steel kettle.

'Let's hope he gets home safely – and soon. Thank you again for your hospitality,' said the Lance-Corporal. He picked up his mug, then went and sat down.

The evenings spent entertaining the soldiers, and days driving for the Red Cross, became a familiar routine. Until, that is, Meldrum was appointed to an important new job. The construction of an aerodrome – a military airport – had been ordered. The new aerodrome was to be built a few miles west of Banff, at a place called Boyndie. There was a need for skilled local drivers to take planners and engineers to and from the site.

So it was that Meldrum found herself becoming the chauffeur for important officials from the Air Ministry, which was in charge of building aerodromes. She picked up the Chief Engineer and the Chief Electrical Engineer from Banff Bridge Railway Station, and drove them up to the aerodrome site. She had two cars to look after and, as well as driving them, she had to keep them in good running order.

Once building work got underway on the aerodrome – intended to be a base from which bomber aircraft would attack

German ships around the North Sea – there was a need for drivers to transport building materials to the site. So Meldrum was called on to undergo another driving test – this time for driving lorries. She passed and was put in charge of three different lorries: a small International Harvester light truck, for running errands around the aerodrome; a Bedford lorry for heavier work; a big Dodge truck, which was used for long journeys hauling heavy loads. With this lorry, Meldrum recalls that the driver had to 'double clutch', which meant that changing gear was a trickier procedure than it would be in a more modern truck.

Driving a big Dodge was daunting enough under any circumstances, but one experience in particular with this truck stuck in Meldrum's mind for ever. It all began when she was ordered to drive to another airstrip at a place called Forres, about 50 miles west of Banff. Her instructions were to pick up a load of fencing wire, which was needed for building the perimeter fence around the new Boyndie aerodrome.

'This consignment of wire weighs too much for one truck-load,' said the man waiting for Meldrum at the Forres airstrip. 'You'll have to do it in two loads.'

Meldrum examined the big coils of wire and thought about the prospect of having to make two journeys instead of one. She replied: 'Yes, but it is not nearly enough for two loads.'

'What do you want to do, then?' the man asked.

'Oh just put it all on,' she said. 'I know I'm overloading, but it should be okay.'

'As you wish,' said the man, and then ordered a team of men to load the big, heavy coils of wire onto the back of the truck.

Meldrum started the engine and put the big truck in gear. She was about to shut the cab door when the man asked: 'Are you sure you will be okay? It looks pretty heavy at the back.'

'Yes, I'll be fine. Don't worry,' she replied, and shut the door before manoeuvring the truck out onto the road.

For several miles, the truck trundled uneventfully along roads that cut through fields and forests. Then, as Meldrum passed the village of Portgordon, the truck began travelling along the coast, through a landscape of beaches, rocky shorelines and cliffs. The road started to get more hilly, and this was when the problems began.

The road became very steep at Cullen, a village which nestled under a grand stone railway viaduct overlooking a pretty harbour. The road took Meldrum's truck into the bottom of the village, near the water. She dropped down the gears and began the long uphill crawl through the arches of the viaduct and the village square.

Suddenly there was a scraping noise from the back of the truck. With the nose of the truck pointing uphill, the big coils of wire had begun slipping to the back of the cargo area. Meldrum felt the steering wheel becoming lighter as the weight in the truck see-sawed towards the rear axle. There was nothing she could do but just press on – onwards and upwards. The men at Boyndie aerodrome were expecting the load to be delivered on time.

Then it happened. Meldrum felt a sensation of weightlessness. The cab of the truck began rising like the basket of a balloon. The hill had become so steep, and the wire had slid so far to the tail of the truck, that the front wheels were lifted off the road.

The truck was now balancing on its rear axle, like a frightened horse up on its hind legs.

At any moment, the truck could topple over. Meldrum could be killed, along with any bystanders. The truck might even roll down the hill and crash into the houses or, worse, the giant stone viaduct. It all seemed certain to end in disaster.

'Oh what am I going to do!?' Meldrum cried out. She felt like panicking, but stopped herself. Instead of losing the plot, she somehow found the courage and common sense needed to turn the situation around. With her heart racing, she carefully worked the pedals and the gear lever to drop the truck into its lowest gear – first – and then slowly let out the clutch. The front wheels settled on the ground and the lorry carried on climbing at a snail's pace. It was going to take her a long time to get to the top of that hill, but at least she would get there in one piece.

After making it to the top of the hill, the truck carried on the few miles to the site of the new aerodrome. A left-hand turn off the main road put Meldrum on the narrow track leading up to the site. Here again was another steep hill. 'I'm not going through all that again,' said Meldrum to herself. So she turned the truck around and reversed up the track instead, ensuring that the load would be balanced safely in the middle of the truck. Still, it was not an easy job to reverse the huge truck for several hundred metres up the narrow, bumpy track.

If any officials from the aerodrome had seen her driving in this way, Meldrum would have been in deep trouble. It was against the rules to reverse up a road like that. Plus, if she had been asked why she was reversing, she would have had to admit that she had dangerously overloaded her lorry.

Without being seen by the guard, Meldrum managed to get her truck turned by the gate to a field, so it was facing the right way before she reached her destination. As she drove past the guard and into the aerodrome where her truck would be unloaded, she felt a huge sense of relief. It had been a really frightening experience.

Once the aerodrome was fully operational, a specialist female support staff arrived on the scene to take on jobs such as driving service cars and trucks. These were the women of the Women's Auxiliary Air Force, or WAAF. Their job was to support the male air crews and ground crews of the Royal Air Force. Yet, despite the arrival of the WAAF, Meldrum was kept on for a long while – perhaps because she had shown her worth as a skilful and hard-working driver. In fact, she stayed on long enough to see the aerodrome – which became known as RAF Banff Strike Wing – change its role from being a place where pilots and crews were trained to being the launch pad for many daring bombing raids on enemy ships in the North Sea and Scandinavia.

Losses among the RAF aircrews were high. The people on the ground nervously counted the number of aircraft returning from a raid to see whether the number was the same as had set out at the beginning of the mission. Sometimes there were quite a few planes missing, and those that did return often had dead or seriously wounded crew members inside their shot-up fuselages.

The Wing Commander, a renowned fighter pilot called Max Aitken, held parties and celebrations at the base to try to keep everyone's spirits up. Meldrum received an invitation to one such celebration, which was a big ball held in honour of a visiting dignitary from the Air Ministry.

On the night of the ball, Meldrum arrived dressed up for the occasion. The airmen and ground staff were all very smart in their RAF uniforms. The smell of hair cream, brass button cleaner and shoe polish mingled with the ever-present cigarette smoke. The WAAF girls wore their hair pinned up and some of them even had nylon stockings that had been smuggled into the camp, since no such stockings could be bought over the counter because of wartime rationing.

A well-known dance band had been brought in to entertain the crowd, and they played the ballroom hits of the day. So far as Meldrum was concerned, though, the real highlight was the food. She had never seen anything like it. A lavish buffet was laid out on tables, with food and drink brought in from far and wide. There was quality turkey and chicken from local farms. There was the finest salmon from local rivers. There was beer, wine and whisky galore. There was exotic fruit, and flowers of all kinds, which had been flown in from the Azores, a faraway group of islands in the Atlantic. In other words, it was all of the things that were ordinarily forbidden because of the strict wartime rationing. Not a powdered egg in sight!

'What a wonderful treat!' Meldrum remarked as she took her place at one of the tables. She had a very memorable night, but as she looked on at the happy faces, she felt a tinge of sadness. The war had been going on for four years, and still she was apart from her husband. At least every successful bombing raid by RAF Banff, against the ships carrying vital enemy supplies from Norway to Germany, brought the conflict closer to an end.

At last, with victory in the Allies' grasp, Meldrum received word that Jack was on his way home. To know that he had survived was a great feeling, but she was apprehensive too. She had not seen him for exactly three years and ten months. Would they be able to pick up where they had left off? They had been married for barely a few weeks before the war tore them apart. Would she even recognize him after all these years?

So much had changed since they had said their last goodbye. She was older and wiser. So many people she knew through the war had come and gone, having either moved away or been killed. Her friend Lydia had got together with a Norwegian soldier, and it looked like they would be married and probably move away to Norway.

By the end of the conflict, Meldrum felt exhausted by the war effort. To add to her other stressful experiences, she had had a close call when a German aircraft flew low over Banff and machine-gunned the street she was on. Luckily a quick-thinking man had grabbed her arm and hauled her into a doorway before she was hit. All of her adventures had taken their toll, and now she longed for a normal and peaceful life.

When the time came, Meldrum got a telephone call. She picked up the receiver from the hook and held it to her ear.

'I've just got back. I'm in Southampton,' said the voice on the other end of the line. It was Jack.

'I'll be up in Edinburgh in a couple of days' time,' he added.

'That will be fine,' she replied.

'You sound a bit funny,' he said. 'Is there something wrong?'

'No . . . well, yes and no,' she said. Before Jack's phone call, she had just received some shocking news. 'I have just been told that my sister nearly drowned off Banff beach today. She swam out of her depth and they had to call the lifeboat and a helicopter.'

'Oh no . . .' said the voice on the phone.

'It's okay,' she reassured him. 'She is in the hospital now, recovering. I'm just a bit upset about it, that's all.'

'Yes, of course,' he said. 'Are we still on for meeting in Edinburgh, then?'

'Yes,' she replied.

'See you in Edinburgh, then.'

That was their agreement. They both took a train to Edinburgh, she from the north and he from the south, and met at a hotel. A hotel room was neutral ground – a quiet and private place, well away from the pressures and expectations of family and friends that would be on them at home.

The couple finally stood in front of each other again, face to face. Jack had changed. He had grown a great big moustache. He was older and more world-weary. Once upon a time his rank had been Second Lieutenant, but during the war he had risen to the high rank of Major. 'My commanding officer was killed so I had to step up,' he said.

She looked at him and smiled.

'You're laughing,' he said, 'What is it?'

'That moustache, it looks funny!' she said.

They both laughed.

'Anyway, what about you? What did you do during the war?' he asked.

'Well . . . I did a bit of driving,' she said.

WAR REPORT

Personnel: Anne Meldrum, Red Cross volunteer and driver from Banff in Aberdeenshire. On the eve of the war, when she was in her mid-twenties, she joined a local detachment of the Red Cross. She was trained to give first aid and perform general nursing duties. She became an ambulance driver then was later appointed as a driver for the Air Ministry to help with the construction of a new aerodrome. Duties included driving key personnel from Banff Bridge Station to the site of the aerodrome at Boyndie, later known as the home of RAF Banff Strike Wing. She was ultimately appointed as a lorry driver at the aerodrome, with three trucks to drive and maintain.

Inventory: The V-series and W-series Dodge trucks. The American truck manufacturer Dodge built a huge range of vehicles during the war for the US Army and its allies, such as the British armed forces. America had a much stronger motor industry than Britain, which was struggling to cope with the war effort, so these imported vehicles were vital. W-series Dodges were used to make ambulances, for example. The truck platform and cab were enhanced by specialist coachwork to create the finished vehicle. A typical Dodge truck used by the RAF was the VK-series. It was a three-ton truck with a long bonnet to cover its long six-cylinder engine. The trucks were loud, dirty and extremely thirsty for petrol – but they got the job done.

Event log: In 1939, the Joint War Organisation was set up to co-ordinate the work of the Red Cross during the war. As a result the British Red Cross, which provided voluntary medical aid during wartime, set up auxiliary hospitals across the country. These hospitals were staffed by trained volunteer nurses to help regular doctors and nurses cope with the number of people wounded because of the war. The volunteer Red Cross nurses were also called on to run canteens for soldiers and to drive ambulances, because the men who would have normally done that job in those days were needed for other wartime duties.

CHAPTER 4

Bombed by Your Own Side

At nine o'clock in the morning, the klaxon went. The sound
from this loud, blaring siren – like a sinister school bell –
filled the grounds of the huge, cube-shaped Duff House. This
house had once been a mansion lived in by aristocratic lords and
ladies, and their servants. It was now a prisoner-of-war camp,
surrounded by an electric barbed-wire fence and machine-gun
emplacements. Anyone who tried to escape would be shot.

The noise brought prisoners in faded military shirts and olive-
coloured trousers streaming out of a door to assemble in a line
on the gravel driveway. A kilted Scottish officer with a neck like a
wrestler barked out their names – 'Ackermann! Houk! Mengelberg!' And so on. Each prisoner after answering his name stood
in silence, except for his own private thoughts.

Thoughts like: why must we always get stale bread and watery
jam for breakfast? Or, if I dug a hole with my spoon when
nobody was looking, how long would it take to tunnel under the
fence and out of here? Or, will I ever see my family again?

And what's that strange, humming noise? Is that why the klaxon was sounded?

The strange, humming noise was coming from above. It was a noise that several of the prisoners recognized. In a funny way, it sounded like home. The prisoners and their guards looked up into the sky as a large, winged object broke through the clouds.

It was an aeroplane, and it was circling low like a huge wasp around the towns of Macduff and Banff. These two Aberdeenshire fishing towns lay on either side of the mouth of the River Deveron. Duff House prisoner-of-war (POW) camp sat on the river's west bank, next to Banff. Adjacent to the house was an arched stone bridge, known as the Brig of Banff, which linked the two towns by crossing the river where it met the sea. The bridge and the prison camp were overlooked from the slope of a hill on the eastern, Macduff, side by Banff Bridge Railway Station.

Some of the people on the ground caught sight of the markings on the aircraft. The Iron Crosses and Swastikas painted on its fuselage and tail marked it out as a fighter-bomber of the German Luftwaffe – a Heinkel 111, to be exact. It had probably come from an airbase across the North Sea in Norway, which was under the control of Nazi Germany.

'It's a Jerry,' thought the Scottish guards to themselves with unease. 'What's he up to?'

'It's one of ours,' thought the German prisoners with surprise. Some of them might even have felt a tinge of relief. Perhaps the plane had come to rescue them?

Then the bombs fell.

German prisoner Paul Mengelberg, standing in the line outside Duff House, was hit by a big blast and then everything went dark. It could have lasted just for a moment, or it could have been for longer. But it was a deathly darkness – the kind of darkness where a person's thoughts can drift off to other times and other places.

Only three weeks previously, Mengelberg had been in the dark and doom-laden atmosphere of a damaged German U-Boat submarine which was sinking powerlessly under the Atlantic Ocean. Somehow, against all the odds, Mengelberg and his fellow crew had got out of that situation alive – and eventually ended up in Duff House POW camp.

Except it looked like now, lying on the gravel outside this Scottish mansion on the morning of Monday, 22 July 1940, after being blown off his feet by the shockwave of a high-explosive bomb, that Mengelberg's luck had finally run out.

It is often said that when facing certain death, a person sees their whole life flash before their eyes. Mengelberg's life had begun in Köln, in northwestern Germany. Like millions of other German teenagers growing up in the 1930s, Mengelberg had believed that the new government led by the Nazi Party of Adolf Hitler was good for Germany. The Nazi government was rebuilding the country and providing jobs for people after Germany's economy and self-confidence had been wrecked when it lost the First World War in 1918.

Mengelberg was exactly the sort of young man who benefited. He did not realise back then that the Nazis would eventually bring shame and misery on Germany. He was trained as an electrician and with his skills he enlisted in the *Kriegsmarine*, or German Navy. He joined the crew of the submarine *U-26*. This U-Boat was launched in 1936 from a port town called Bremen, which lies on the River Weser in northwest Germany, leading to the North Sea. There were 48 men in the crew and everyone had an important job to do. Mengelberg was an electrical engineer.

The *U-26* was a Type 1A U-Boat. Mengelberg and his fellow crew found the conditions aboard ship cramped and inhospitable. The vessel was sent to sea for weeks or even months at a time. Food on a U-Boat was typically packed into every corner, even being piled up in the spare toilet. Bread and fruit had to be eaten quickly before they went bad, which left the men with only tinned food for the rest of the mission.

Showers, baths and shaving were not allowed. The men grew long beards and smelled terrible, even though they used primitive deodorants. The air stank of body odours, fishy and salty seawater, and diesel from the fuel tanks and engines. Only for short periods when the U-Boat was on the surface could the men climb out onto the deck and see daylight, and get some fresh air. Even then, however, their feet were not on dry land and all they could see was the cold, grey sea.

Life on a U-Boat wasn't just dirty, dark and depressing. It was dangerous. So it was a good idea for a sailor to have life insurance, in case he was injured or killed. This meant your family would not lose out financially if you died. On one occasion while the vessel put ashore, the crew of the *U-26* were visited by a man selling life insurance. Little did they realise that this man was in fact an undercover British spy, gathering information about the U-Boats, their crew, and their missions. Like other members of the crew, the young Mengelberg unwittingly revealed details about himself and his work to the insurance salesman.

The spy had to gather as much information as possible because the British government was worried about what the

Germans were up to. Building U-Boats and sending them out to patrol the oceans were all part of a process in Germany called 're-armament'. After Germany lost the First World War back in 1918 it had not been allowed to build new weapons, tanks or warships. But things were changing rapidly. The Nazi government had started to build new weapons so it could re-arm the country.

Why? Well, as it turned out, Hitler and the Nazis wanted to take back land and sea territory they had lost during the First World War, and they were prepared to go to war again for it if necessary.

Hitler didn't stop there, though. While the *Kriegsmarine* U-Boats such as the *U-26* prowled the seas on training exercises and patrols, the land army soon got busy conquering Germany's neighbours – countries such as Austria and Poland. In some places, things got brutal and bloody. On 3 September 1939 the British government decided enough was enough and declared war on Germany. It was the moment everyone had been expecting, and dreading: a second world war was about to begin. Hitler now ordered his forces to attack the British.

The crew of *U-26* received orders to sink as many ships as possible belonging to Britain and its Allies. Under various captains, including Heinz Scheringer, the *U-26* got its teeth into the enemy and was deadly during the first few months of the war. It sank eleven ships and damaged two more. By the summer of 1940, the Atlantic Ocean had become a happy hunting ground for Mengelberg and his comrades.

Then, on 30 June 1940, disaster struck. While sailing off the west coast of Ireland, the *U-26* had tracked down an Allied convoy. At first it looked like Scheringer and his crew could notch up some more unsuspecting victims. The U-Boat needed to dive to prepare for a torpedo attack, but when it did so it was spotted by the Allies.

As the submarine dived beneath the surface its engines chose this crucial moment to cut out, ruining the chances of a quick retreat. This is perhaps why only two Type 1A U-Boats were ever built – the design was said to be unreliable and it had poor manoeuvrability. While Mengelberg and his colleagues cursed their rotten luck, the *U-26* was intercepted by HMS *Gladiolus*, the convoy's British escort corvette. The crew of the *U-26* did manage to torpedo one of the ships in the convoy before crash-diving to try to evade the *Gladiolus*.

The *Gladiolus* dropped depth charges over the submerged U-Boat. These barrel-shaped bombs were timed to explode at a set depth to try to destroy a submarine, or damage it and force it to the surface. A number of these charges exploded around the *U-26* at a depth of about 80 metres, which is the depth of 40 swimming pools on top of each other, and the underwater shock waves terrified the crew and caused the vessel's pressure hull to flex and then rupture. This meant that seawater was able to get in and the U-Boat began flooding at the stern, which was the back end of the boat. The *U-26* was left without adequate power, without lights and sinking uncontrollably.

Mengelberg and his comrades looked at the clock-shaped depth gauge, which showed how deep the submarine was going. They all knew that the maximum safe depth for a Type 1A U-Boat was 100 metres. If it sank deeper than that, the chances of being crushed by the pressure of the seawater got bigger and bigger until – BANG! – the *U-26* and its crew would be splattered like an egg in an angry wrestler's fist.

The needle went round the gauge until it reached 'Maximum'. Then it kept on going and broke the pin that was supposed to prevent it going any further. All eyes were fixed on the needle as it carried on round the dial. Some of the men mopped the sweat from their brows with their shirtsleeves. They hardly dared to look. The metal hull made creaking noises as the stress on it grew more and more.

Eventually, the boat settled at a depth of 230 metres – more than twice the safe operational depth. The stern was now full of water and the doors between compartments could not be shut. The pressure of the water against the hull outside was so severe that the interior bulkheads – the walls between compartments – were bent out of shape, and so were the doorframes. The whole boat was in darkness, with only emergency lights on.

The men wanted to scream, but everyone knew the order from Captain Scheringer: 'Absolute silence.' Staying completely silent was the crew's only chance of survival. Even a loud cough or a footstep might create enough of a sound that when amplified by the echoing hull could be picked up hundreds of metres away by the *Gladiolus*'s special underwater sound detection equipment, known as ASDIC.

Hours went by as the *U-26* lay deep underwater, absolutely silent.

'He's playing the same game,' thought Mengelberg to himself as he looked up and wondered about the *Gladiolus*. The captains of both vessels were trying to fool each other into thinking that each had gone away. The hope of the submarine crew was that the *Gladiolus* would believe the *U 26* had been sunk, and then leave the area. Meanwhile the corvette was trying to convince the enemy below that it had given up the hunt and sailed off.

Eventually, Captain Scheringer decided to take his chances. There was no way the submarine could stay submerged much longer. The men would run out of oxygen and asphyxiate. The order was given to blow the ballast tanks, which caused pressurized air to fill up the tanks and make the submarine lighter, or more buoyant, than the water around it. The U-26 began rising to the surface. Nobody on board could afford to feel relieved, though. Who knew what was waiting for them up there?

When the U-26 broke the surface, it may have seemed at first as though the coast was clear. Just as it tried to limp away, however, the German submarine was spotted again – this time from the air. The Allies had in fact called in their best weapon – a Short Sunderland flying boat patrol bomber. This aeroplane, which took off and landed on water, was specially designed to hunt submarines.

The Sunderland swooped over the U-26. As the submarine attempted to crash-dive below the surface, the aircraft dropped four anti-submarine bombs, each weighing 113kg. The U-26 was crippled and incapable of escape. Captain Scheringer realised the situation was now hopeless. He and his crew were compelled to choose either a watery grave or else abandon ship. They chose the latter.

The submarine sat still on the surface of the waves as a Royal Navy destroyer called HMS *Rochester* arrived on the scene. Mengelberg and the rest of the exhausted and bedraggled German crew were picked up off the deck safely. Captain Scheringer scuttled the ship, leaving it to sink. As the last men were taken off, the U-26 disappeared below the waves for ever.

The Germans were put ashore on British soil and then

interrogated in London. The men may have expected a grilling from British intelligence officers, with lots of hard questions and tough talking. They were not prepared for what actually happened, though.

'Remember me?' said the intelligence officer as Mengelberg sat down for his interview. It was the insurance salesman who had visited *U-26* before the war! Now his true identity was revealed – and Mengelberg knew he must have gathered all sorts of useful information while he was spying. The officer joked that, thanks to the success of the British spying operation, there was hardly any need for Mengelberg to be interviewed again now.

After the interrogation, Mengelberg and other members of the *U-26* crew were put on a train that would take them to the opposite end of Britain – Scotland's northeast coast. Destination: Duff House Prisoner of War Camp. The men were marched from Banff Bridge Railway Station, over the bridge itself, and into the grounds of the house.

'It's all so green,' said Mengelberg to one of the others, as they trudged over the grass pastures and passed under the boughs of the leafy trees. The electric fence around the grounds was about two-and-a-half metres high, with guards patrolling it.

When Mengelberg and the others passed through the gate, they were met by a big, muscular Scottish Sergeant-Major who furiously barked orders at them. 'He's a real ramrod, he's going to be tough,' said one of the others to Mengelberg. The Sergeant-Major soon earned the nickname of 'The Neck-Shooter' because of the way he spat out orders like a machine gun.

It was not difficult for the new arrivals to imagine that Duff House had once been an elegant stately home, finely furnished and decorated. Now, however, it was stripped to its bare bones and the prisoners would find no luxuries inside. Mengelberg was marched up a stone spiral staircase to his quarters on an upper floor of the building.

For dinner each evening the prisoners were served mutton and potatoes. In the morning, for breakfast, they were given one slice of bread served with watered-down jam in Army mess tins, which were deep metal dishes. Mengelberg learned to dip his bread on one side and then turn it over until the whole slice was soaked and mushy. Then he dug it all out with his spoon and hungrily guzzled it.

'Only pigs eat like this,' Mengelberg remarked to one of his fellow prisoners. But he didn't mind so much. At least they were alive, and they could eat. Plus they could learn a famous British tradition: tea drinking. The prisoners were served tea galore.

The peace and quiet of a summer morning on the Banffshire coast must have suggested to at least some of the POWs that they were now a long way away from the dangers of the ocean's front line. Yet survival even here could not be taken for granted. Especially not on the morning of Monday, 22 July, when a Heinkel 111 was speeding low over the North Sea at around 250 miles per hour, heading in their direction.

The attacking aircraft began dropping its bombs just after nine o'clock. The bombs fell on Macduff. They fell on the river, narrowly missing what seemed to be their intended targets of the bridge and the railway station, and they fell on the grounds of Duff House.

Two bombs dropped straight through the skylight window over the lift shaft in the centre of the house. They turned out to be duds, and didn't go off – otherwise the main part of the house would surely have been destroyed. Still, the damage to the east wing of the house was bad enough. This wing was an extension that had been added during Victorian times. It was hit and caught fire, with smoke and steam pouring from it.

It was one of the bombs landing outside that knocked Mengelberg off his feet. When he opened his eyes, he was quite amazed to discover that he was still alive.

Too dazed and groggy to notice that the plane had finished its attack and flown away, Mengelberg ran inside the building. His mind was a blur and he didn't know what he was doing. As he stood in the entrance, he came within an inch of being killed for a third time in as many weeks. The windowed door had been shocked by the blast, with all its glass shattered and its hinges and frame weakened. At the precise moment the German sailor passed through it, the door fell down upon him. Miraculously, the glassless hole of the window fell right neatly over him and he was able to step out of the door unscathed.

Less fortunate was Mengelberg's comrade Hans Houk. He had been standing with his back to the window when the bombs blew up outside. Now he was lying on the ground, with his back plastered with shards of glass from the window. It had shattered with great force as a result of shockwaves from the high-explosive bombs.

As the clouds of smoke and steam rose through the trees, the scene of devastation at Duff House could be made out by Banff residents living in nearby houses. Some of these families believed they would be hit too, but in the event they escaped relatively unscathed. The chief casualties were broken windows, along with ornaments and pictures that crashed to the floor, echoing the half-a-dozen or so loud bangs that were heard as each live bomb hit the ground.

There were some locals injured, though, since the slaughter-house at Macduff had been hit along with other civilian areas. These people would soon be taken to the local Chalmers Hospital, just off Banff High Street, for treatment. In the meantime, ambulances and the local auxiliary fire service converged on the grounds of Duff House, where surviving prisoners helped the fire and ambulance crews get to grips with the carnage.

'Did you see what kind of plane it was?' said one prisoner to the Allied officer who was kneeling down beside him. The prisoner's name was Ackermann. His torso, or main body, was ripped in two. Ackermann carried on talking clearly to the officer comforting him, even though he was now only half a person. Then, all of a sudden, Ackermann died.

In total six German prisoners died in the bombing, and so did two of their Scottish guards. The wounded were rushed to the Chalmers Hospital.

As the casualties suddenly rushed in, the scene at the hospital was very confused and chaotic. Enemy prisoners had to be tended to in beds side by side with local civilians. For security reasons patients would have to be sorted into proper groups – but the top priority was to treat people and prevent any further fatalities.

'*Haben Sie Deutsch, vielleicht?*' A local woman who knew some German was trying to speak to one of the prisoners so she could translate for the doctor who would be treating him. The man just ignored her.

She tried again. '*Entschuldigung, sind Sie Deutsch vielleicht?*'

The man carried on ignoring her and seemed to grow irritated. Then a thought struck the doctor.

'Which part of Germany are you from?' he asked in English.

'I'm nae from Germany!' said the man finally in a strong Banffshire accent. 'I'm local!'

Eventually a separate ward was set up for the prisoners and staffed by nurses from the local detachment of the Red Cross, a special medical organisation for treating war wounded. The ward was put under armed guard.

As the nurses went about their business, they exchanged news about what had happened. One nurse had been cycling towards Banff Bridge when the bomber appeared overhead. When the bombs fell and exploded, she thought a group of local boys standing nearby had been hit, since she saw one of them collapse. Luckily it was due to shock, nothing more. She led the three lads into a tunnel beside the bridge so they could shelter from any possible further attack before pedalling off to help treat the wounded.

One of the most severely wounded prisoners on the ward was a fellow named Herbert Büschel. His entire body was cut by shrapnel – small, nasty pieces of jagged metal that were packed into the bombs to make them as deadly as possible. For many hours, Büschel was in the operating theatre where the doctors and nurses worked to save him.

'We removed one piece of shrapnel for every day of the year from that man. That's 365 pieces,' said the Ward Sister when Büschel was wheeled out of the operating theatre with his entire body covered in bandages, like he was an Egyptian mummy. There were just a few small holes cut in the bandages for his eyes, nose and mouth. At first, it was believed that the German would probably not survive – but eventually he began to get better.

One of the prisoners played a tune on a mouth organ he had been given as a gift from a local family. The sound of a sad German ballad called 'Die Lorelei' floated across the ward. It is a song about a siren, or mermaid, who lies on a rock and lures sailors to their deaths. It seemed to reflect the ironic fact it was on dry land, rather than in the sea, that the dead U-Boat sailors had met their end.

The patients got to know quite well the nurses who were treating them. The prisoners showed photographs of their families back in Germany – girlfriends, wives and children. The Germans also wrote notes and letters of thanks to the hospital staff. One wrote in German: *'Ein herzliches Dankechön . . . die ich nie vergessen werde.'* The words translated as: 'My heartfelt thanks, I will never forget you.'

Word spread on the ward that the bomber had tried to make its escape back across the North Sea. People learned that two Spitfire fighter aircraft were launched from RAF Dyce airfield near Aberdeen. The Heinkel was intercepted and shot down.

Meanwhile, as preparations were made to move the prisoners to a more secure location until the war was over, Mengelberg and the others were left wondering: why us? Why had the German Luftwaffe decided to attack fellow Germans in this quiet corner of Scotland?

'I think it must have been a reconnaissance aircraft,' said one prisoner. 'The pilot saw all the Allied troops down below, the barbed-wire fences around this big house, and he thought to himself – "Let's teach them a lesson".'

Another prisoner lit a cigarette and a puff of smoke rose up over his bandaged head as he replied, 'Ja, I think you're right. They must be flying lots of missions off the Scottish coast, bombing the British ships and spying on their coastal defences. He probably thought this was an important base full of Allied soldiers. A good target.'

Mengelberg thought about the six comrades who had been killed by the wrong side because of the pilot's mistake. It was cruel and ironic to die at the hands of friends instead of enemies. 'They survived fighting Allied ships in the deadly Atlantic and got out of the submarine safe and sound,' he said. 'Then a German bomber comes here and kills them. That is hard to take!'

The others agreed. 'Ja, that is hard to take.'

WAR REPORT

Personnel: Paul Mengelberg was born in Köln, also known as Cologne, in 1916. He trained as an electrician and joined the *Kriegsmarine* – the German navy – as a U-Boat sailor. His boat was the *U-26*. After the war broke out the crew were successful against the Allies, until eventually being captured on 1 July 1940 off the coast of Ireland. The crew were taken to London for interrogation, with Mengelberg and others then transported by train to Duff House POW Camp in Banff, Scotland. After the camp was bombed by the Luftwaffe on 22 July 1940 the prisoners were transferred to England and then to Canada, where Mengelberg remained in custody until the war was over. After the war, which ended in victory for Britain and the Allies, Mengelberg returned to Germany. He found his native city of Köln had been utterly destroyed in air raids by RAF Lancaster bombers, which are discussed elsewhere in this book. Mengelberg saw that there was nothing left for him at home so he returned to Canada. He found work as an engineer and settled down in Ontario to bring up a family.

Event log: The air raid on Banff and Macduff in July 1940 was a reflection of a much larger strategic attack by the German Luftwaffe which was going on across Western Europe, especially in larger towns and cities. This major attack, which went on for months, is often referred to as the Blitzkrieg, or Blitz. The word Blitzkrieg is German for 'lightning war' and the idea behind it was to attack the enemy so quickly and with such force using tanks, troops, warships and aircraft that he would be totally overwhelmed. Even though the attacks in quiet rural places like Banff were opportunistic and quite isolated, unlike the heavy bombing of places like Clydebank or London, they still had the effect of making the people on the ground afraid of the mighty German war machine. In fact, villages and towns in the northeast of Scotland near Banff were bombed heavily considering their small population, with important seaports such as Fraserburgh, Peterhead and Aberdeen badly damaged and a lot of people killed. Duff House was lucky to escape total destruction. The east wing had to be demolished, and the building that remains still has visible blast marks on its exterior walls.

Inventory: The *U-26* was a Type 1A U-Boat of the German navy, known as the *Kriegsmarine*. This U-Boat was built by a company called A. G. Weser, at a shipyard on the Weser River at Bremen in northwest Germany. The vessel was launched in the spring of 1936 and sailed down the river to the North Sea. The *U-26* was about 73 metres long and its displacement – which means weight – was about 900 tonnes. It was designed for a crew of 43 but there were 48 men on it when it was captured in 1940. The Type 1A U-Boat was an attack submarine carrying 14 torpedoes, with a gun on the deck, among other weapons. It communicated secretly with the rest of the German navy using a device with a keyboard called an Enigma machine. Besides using this machine, the *Kriegsmarine* were careful to apply a lot of other special codes and procedures that made it especially hard for the Allies to work out what the U-Boats were up to. Only two Type 1A U-Boats were built. The other one was *U-25*, which hit a mine in the North Sea a month after the *U-26* was captured. The *U-25* was sunk with the loss of all hands. The U-Boat crews were very successful against the Allies, but on the other hand they suffered a 75 per cent casualty rate. This meant a U-Boat crewman had only a 1 in 4 chance of coming home alive. It made life in the U-Boats the most dangerous of all the German forces.

CHAPTER 5
Enemy Alien

A shadowy, black vehicle cruised slowly along the road under the gloom of a forest canopy. Its two large, round headlamps were on, but they were dim and odd-looking. The lenses were covered with black material, except for a narrow slit in each that let out only a ribbon of light.

The lamps were mounted over large curved mudguards, and between them was a tall chrome grille behind which a straight six-cylinder petrol engine burbled and roared with each change of gear. The grille had two emblems on it. Near the top was a small, oval-shaped decal bearing the name of the car's British manufacturer – Wolseley – in elegant script. At the bottom of the grille was a much larger sign bearing the word: 'POLICE'.

The police car continued west along the main Deeside road from Aberdeen until it entered the village of Aboyne and turned north up a smaller road. After a while it turned off this road, too, and followed a track into the grounds of a secluded country mansion.

As with the car headlamps, the windows of the house were covered up to obey the blackout regulations. It was the early summer of 1940. Nazi Germany seemed to have conquered most of Europe and the enemy was now on Britain's doorstep. The Luftwaffe threatened to bomb from the skies during the night. In order to hide any potential targets, every trace of light on the ground had to be covered up – or blacked out – as much as possible.

The car pulled up on the gravel outside and two policemen got out. They adjusted their caps as they walked to the door and rang the bell.

The door was answered by a woman in nurse's uniform.

'Good afternoon, Sister,' said one of the policemen. 'We are sorry to trouble you on a Sunday, but we are here to see Mrs Löwit, the cook.'

The woman nodded.

'Actually, we would like to speak to Mrs Löwit's son, Hans Löwit,' said the second policeman. 'We believe he is here from Aberdeen visiting his mother.'

A short while later the car was on its way back to police headquarters in Aberdeen. In the back seat sat a young man dressed in his Sunday-best clothes, nervously looking at the uniformed men next to him.

'We are sorry to have upset your mother but we had to take you into custody, Hans,' said one of the policemen. 'Now that our troops have had to retreat from France and Hitler has us in his gunsights, the British government can't run the risk of having any enemy aliens on the loose.'

'Enemy aliens' were men who had settled in Scotland but whose original homes were in countries now fighting with Nazi

Germany against Britain in the war. Since Löwit came from one such country, Austria, the police now had orders to arrest and imprison him.

As the car motored through the beautiful countryside, Löwit wondered what was waiting for him around the corner. He consoled himself by remembering that things could be a lot worse. In fact the type of men in uniform taking him away could have been of a far, far worse sort had he and his mother failed to escape from Austria in the nick of time.

After he left school in Vienna, Austria's capital city, Löwit had done well enough in his exams to enrol as a medical student. The University of Vienna was a fine place to study to be a doctor, and in ordinary times it would have been a great place to be a young man about town. But this was no ordinary time.

In March 1938, a dramatic event happened called the *Anschluss*. It meant that Austria lost its independence. The country was joined up with its nextdoor neighbour, Germany, to become part of Greater Germany. Hitler, the leader of Nazi Germany, and his entourage rolled through the historic centre of Vienna in a fleet of black, supercharged eight-cylinder Mercedes-Benz 770K limousines.

These huge open-topped cars, built in Stuttgart, were an awesome symbol of German power and prestige, and they threatened to mow down anyone who got in their way. Hitler, known as the Führer, waved proudly and triumphantly to crowds of tens of thousands of Austrian people who packed the pavements and cheered while giving enthusiastic, straight-armed Nazi salutes.

Löwit did not cheer the Nazis. He knew they would not want him to, anyway. In fact, now that Hitler was in control of Vienna, it was not even safe for young men like Löwit to be out on the street.

The Löwit family were Jews. This meant that from now on their lives were in grave danger. The Nazis and their followers despised Jewish people. Support for the Nazis was so strong in Vienna that Jews found themselves bullied, harassed and beaten up at every turn by uniformed Nazi police and their eager supporters. It seemed like the whole city was against the Jews.

'I'm just going out to meet my pal, Mum,' Löwit said to his mother one afternoon.

'Make sure you go on your bike, Hans!' said his mother in a fearful tone of voice.

Cycling was safer than walking. A bike made it harder for Nazi thugs to catch you than if you were on foot. As Löwit pedalled through the town to meet his friend, Hans Baader, he could see how badly Jewish people were being treated.

Everyone seemed to be under Hitler's thumb, and had to do exactly as he dictated. Either fearfully or willingly, they did as they were told. Tram drivers were even ordered by the new Nazi government to stop driving on the left-hand side of the road and start driving on the right instead.

The change of driving side might have seemed trivial, but other new rules were not. The drivers and conductors also had orders to ban all Jews from riding on the trams. Löwit saw Jewish families being shoved off trams or ignored by drivers as they waited at the stops.

'NO JEWS ALLOWED. JEWS FORBIDDEN.' There were signs like this all over the place. Jews were not permitted to go to the park. They were not allowed to go to the cinema. They were not allowed to go to the swimming pool. Everywhere you looked, the message was clear.

Löwit saw a Jewish man on his hands and knees, ordered to scrub the street to make it nice and clean for non-Jews. 'We're not even second-class citizens,' Löwit said to himself angrily. 'We are the dregs!'

'Have you seen how everyone is wearing a Swastika on their lapel?' asked Baader when Löwit met his friend.

'Yes,' said Löwit. 'They have all become ardent Nazis. What are we going to do?'

The two friends were angry and frightened. But they refused to be treated like slaves. They decided to show their defiance by wearing a symbol of their own. Instead of a Swastika, which Jews were banned from wearing anyway, they each attached a yellow dandelion to their lapels.

The flower was a symbol of peace, and it was a way of quietly mocking the Nazis. But Löwit and Baader knew it made them more of a target for the Jew-haters. As they stepped out onto the street together, they held their heads up high and tried to ignore the malevolent stares of Nazi supporters on every corner, but it was only a matter of time before these two young Jewish men would be beaten to a pulp – or worse.

'We have to get out,' said Löwit's mother finally one day.

'But we can't get out,' replied her son. 'No other countries want to let us in!'

'I think I have found a way,' she said. 'Go and fetch your passport.'

Löwit's mother was a cook and a housekeeper, and luckily knew a number of sympathetic and well-connected non-Jews. She had been put in touch with the Quaker Church, which was an international organisation whose members bravely opposed bullying and violence wherever it happened. The Quakers were working to give Jews a passage out of dangerous Nazi areas by finding them jobs in safe countries.

In December 1938, Löwit's passport was taken, along with his mother's, to a bureau and presented to an official at a desk. The cover of the passport read 'THIRD REICH REISEPASS' and inside were Löwit's photograph, date of birth and other details. Unlike other passports of the so-called Greater Germany, this one had been stamped with a big, blood-red letter J – for Jew.

There was a loud thump as the official hit the booklet with a new stamp and handed the passport back. When Löwit opened it, he saw his ticket to freedom. The stamp read:

'Visa For United Kingdom'.

Under it were the handwritten words 'For Domestic Employment'.

The Quakers had arranged jobs for Löwit and his mother in a faraway place they had never been to before – Scotland. Löwit turned his thoughts to packing his belongings and closed his passport. It was the end of one chapter and the beginning of another.

Several months later, Löwit was striding across a Scottish moor with a large picnic hamper slung over his shoulder. It contained lunch for Colonel Lilburn and his friends.

Colonel Lilburn was Löwit's new boss. The Quakers had found Löwit work as a butler and handyman in the Colonel's mansion, called Coull House, and on the Colonel's estate – a large area of land where the Colonel went shooting grouse, a Scottish game bird.

Coull House was near Aboyne, a village in Deeside, which was a part of the eastern Highlands of Scotland on the edge of the Cairngorm mountains. The area got its name because the River Dee flows through it. Queen Victoria often came to this region to relax and hunt during the nineteenth century – and it remained very popular among aristocrats and well-off people for shooting and fishing.

When he wasn't traipsing across country at the Colonel's beck and call, Löwit was working in and around Coull House. It was here that his mother, too, worked for the Colonel and his wife. Mrs Löwit was a cook – and a very good one, too.

For some reason Mrs Lilburn thought it would be nice for her young Austrian handyman to learn to do something other than heavy lifting, fixing and cleaning. So she tried to teach Löwit flower arranging. She was not very successful, but at least it passed the time.

Another way of marking time was Löwit's weekly visit to the local police station in Aboyne. It was a condition of his being allowed to stay in Britain that he presents himself to the authorities each week, so they could check that he was working as he should be and that everything was in order. It was an easy visit. Löwit got to know the policemen quite well. After a few simple checks he was free to go.

On one occasion, though, things were different. It was September 1939 and Britain had declared war on Germany after Hitler invaded another one of Germany's neighbours – Poland. It now looked like the Führer wanted to conquer all of Europe. The policeman, who was hunched over the counter, looked up as Löwit came in the door to the police station.

'What's this I hear about you, Hans?' said the uniformed man, resting his fists on the counter. 'You are telling people that everything will be better when Hitler gets here?'

'Huh?!' said Löwit with surprise. His chest began to tighten. He was gripped by fear as the policeman eyed him steadily. He knew that if the authorities here suspected he was a Nazi he would be arrested on the spot, and might even be shot for treason.

Next to the counter, on the wall, was a shiny poster from the new Ministry of Information. It was about the war. It read: 'Careless Talk Costs Lives!'

Löwit had to think fast. Then it came back to him. He had recently had a conversation with a local farmer. The farmer was complaining about how terrible it was that Britain had to go to war. Löwit, thinking that it was right for Britain to go to war to try to stop the Nazis, had replied: 'Anything is better than Hitler getting here!'

The policeman listened to the explanation, delivered in Löwit's German-sounding Austrian accent. 'The farmer must have misunderstood me,' Löwit added, and then waited nervously for the constable's response.

'Very well,' said the policeman eventually. 'And how's your mother?'

The moment of danger had passed. Löwit felt a tremendous sense of relief.

Back at Coull House, the war meant that things were changing fast. The Colonel was called up right away for military duty. The house itself was requisitioned – taken over by the government – and turned into a maternity hospital. This was a special hospital where women from the City of Glasgow could come to give birth in a place that would be safe from the attention of German airforce bombers.

Löwit's mother's cooking skills were needed more than ever, so she was welcome to stay. As for her son, on the other hand, the authorities wanted him to move out. Löwit needed to get a job and a place to stay elsewhere. Because of where he came from, Löwit was unlikely to be welcomed by many other employers. Once again, though, the Quakers came to his rescue.

The Church helped Löwit to find work and get his medical studies back on track. He got some work as a trainee in the X-Ray Department of Aberdeen Royal Infirmary, a teaching hospital about 30 miles east of Aboyne. He lodged with a very kind lady called Mrs Hall on Albert Street, near the centre of Aberdeen.

It was now the winter of 1939–40. Although Löwit was getting some training at the hospital, for the rest of the time he was unemployed. To keep himself useful and active, he found a job shovelling snow to keep the city's roads and pavements clear. It was a strange reminder of the street-cleaning Jews had had to do in Vienna, except in Aberdeen you were treated well and it was a proper job.

In the early part of 1940, the dark winter months were reflected by bad news about the war. The German forces seemed unstoppable as they advanced further and further across Europe. Between April and June, huge areas of the continent from Scandinavia in the north to France and the Mediterranean in the south fell under Nazi control. The British tried to stop the Germans by sending a British Expeditionary Force (BEF) of tens of thousands of men across the English Channel. But the BEF was defeated, and had to evacuate from a place on the French coast called Dunkirk.

There was a national panic in Britain. People thought that it was only a matter of time before this country, too, fell into Nazi hands. As a result, the authorities wanted to take all measures necessary to stop that happening. One of the precautions was to lock up all male 'enemy aliens' living in the UK, just in case they decided to fight for Hitler by causing sabotage or other mayhem. As Prime Minister Winston Churchill put it, the government's policy was to 'Collar the lot!'

This was when the police car tracked Löwit down one weekend while he was visiting his mother at Coull House, and 'collared' him.

Löwit was taken to the police headquarters on Lodge Walk, where he met about a dozen other 'enemy aliens' like himself living in Aberdeen or the surrounding area. Löwit spent the night in a police cell and was kept a prisoner in Scotland for about a week. He was then transported by train to a place in England called Huyton, near Liverpool. The prison camp at Huyton was a housing estate that was just being built, and had been converted into a prison camp with barbed-wire fences and armed guards.

After three months in Huyton, in August 1940 Löwit and many other 'enemy aliens' were shipped across the Atlantic Ocean to Canada, a country that supported the British. The voyage was dangerous because German U-Boats were lying in wait off the coast, ready to hunt down any ships they could find belonging to Britain or its Allies. One vessel carrying enemy aliens had been sunk a month earlier with the loss of hundreds of lives. Luckily, Löwit's ship made it safely across the water.

The camp in Canada was a huge railway shed, holding 500 men. It was heated by steam. In the winter Canada was exceedingly cold, so a lot of time was spent out in the forests chopping down trees for wood to fuel the boiler that made the steam. The prison guards were Canadian veterans of the First World War. They did not take very seriously the idea that young Jewish men such as Löwit, or other prisoners, including many who had fought against the Nazis at home for political reasons, were truly a threat to the Allies.

'Here, hold this,' said the guard to one of the prisoners, as a group of them stood in the snow amid a forest of huge trees. Löwit and the others watched with slight amazement as the guard handed the prisoner his rifle – the rifle he was supposed to shoot if any of them tried to escape. The guard was freezing after standing still for so long while the others worked. So to warm himself up, he picked up an axe and began furiously chopping wood. Nobody tried to escape.

The Canadian camps were well organized and many of the people there were highly skilled – doctors, teachers, engineers, scientists, writers, artists, businesspeople — you name it. They even held classes in the camps so that people could continue their education despite being imprisoned. Plus you could do some work and get paid for it, allowing you to save a bit of money. Löwit worked as a plumber.

Eventually the British authorities admitted what they had privately known all along: men like Löwit were the last people on earth who would want to help Hitler win the war. So in late 1942, after about two years in captivity, Löwit was told that he could volunteer to join the British army and join the fight against the Nazis – which is exactly what he did.

He boarded a boat to take him back across the Atlantic to Scotland. After evading the deadly groups of U-Boats, known as 'Wolf Packs', the ship arrived in Greenock, near Glasgow.

Löwit returned south to Huyton, which was now an army

camp. He was inducted into the British Army, and given leave – a holiday – before he would be sent to fight on the front line against the German Army. He was no longer an 'enemy alien' and for the duration of his leave, for the first time since he was a boy, he felt completely free.

'What a great feeling it is to sit here with ordinary people,' Löwit said to himself as he watched the Scottish countryside roll by from the comfort of his train carriage. Once again he was heading to Coull House, to see his mother. Except this time there would be no sinister knock at the door.

When he arrived back at Coull House, Löwit introduced himself as Ian. The British Army had required him to change his identity by anglicizing his name, so that he sounded less like one of the enemy. From now on his full name was Ian Lowit. Goodbye Hans Löwit.

Lowit's first job in the army was with the Pioneer Corps, building special mobile bridges. After a while, though, he was permitted to volunteer for the regular army. He became an anti-tank gunner.

After the swarms of landing craft arrived on the beaches of northwest France on D-Day, which was a huge counter-attack against the Germans by Britain and the Allies, Lowit was sent to join in the fight. It was 1944 and the Germans were now on the back foot, but far from beaten.

'Watch out for enemy patrols,' said a commanding officer. Lowit was in the 62nd anti-tank regiment in Belgium. The vehicle towing their heavy gun was so cumbersome and slow that they could not keep up with the front line of the attack that was pushing the Germans back.

So Lowit and his comrades in 247 Anti-Tank Battery were

forced to join the rear of the Allied advance. They went on patrol looking for German soldiers still in the area. They also cleared debris from the roads, and helped villagers sort out the ruins left behind by the fighting.

'Everyone gather round,' said one of Löwit's comrades when they were parked up in a Belgian village. 'Let's take a photograph.' The men of 247 Anti-Tank Battery clambered on to the back of their gun's towing vehicle, a Crusader tank chassis, along with a number of villagers. They sat and posed together in a moment that celebrated the liberation of the village from the Nazis. Among the locals was a pretty young girl, who smiled as the handsome young soldier next to her put an arm around her shoulder.

'What's your name?' the girl asked.

'It's a long story,' he replied. 'But you can call me Ian.'

As winter set in, Lowit found himself walking with his rifle along a massive wall, or dyke, surrounded by floodwater on a Belgian island. He and his comrades were on a patrol while the retreating Germans occupied another island about two miles away. The dykes had been built to reclaim dry land from the sea. But before abandoning the island, the Germans had deliberately flooded it by blasting holes in the dykes.

It all seemed strangely peaceful. In fact it was deadly if you were unlucky. Another troop of Lowit's battery were found one morning with their throats cut by a night-time German patrol – except for one lad who had managed to escape. He was straggling behind the others and was not seen by the Germans because he was crouching down to tie his bootlace.

Some of Lowit's encounters had been heartwarming and other episodes were chilling – but all were a reminder of why the war was worth fighting and why the Nazis had to be defeated. And defeated they were, eventually, when the Nazi capital of Berlin was captured by the Allies, and Victory in Europe was declared on VE Day – 8 May, 1945.

Peace had come too late, though, for many of the people Lowit had left behind. Vienna was now in ruins after it had been bombarded by the Allies to drive the Nazis out. Lowit decided that he would return to Scotland, where his mother had now settled, and begin a new life there. But first he wanted to learn what had become of his best friend, Hans Baader.

Lowit discovered that Baader had escaped to Slovakia, a country next to Austria, to seek refuge with relatives. But Slovakia was soon conquered by Hitler, too. On 9 March 1942, it was decreed that all Jews in Slovakia had to wear a Yellow Star badge with the word 'Jew' written on it in big black letters. A week later, the Nazis began transporting Jews in Slovakia to death camps where all of them – men, women and children – were executed by being poisoned with gas.

Baader was among those captured and killed by the Nazis. Across Europe, millions of Jews and hundreds of thousands of other people hated by the Nazis were murdered in an event known as the Holocaust. It was only by a stroke of good luck that Lowit and his mother had escaped to Scotland before it was too late. Yet, if Britain had fallen to the Nazis, they probably would have been gassed too.

Before he died, Baader had been made to wear the Yellow Star like the other Jews. Lowit remembered how, back in 1938, the two friends had attached dandelions to their lapels and walked defiantly around the streets of Vienna with their homemade symbols.

Symbols on clothes had been occasionally used since medieval times to mark Jews out as different. Yet the two friends could have had no idea what the Nazis had in store when they made their own yellow badges. It was as though they had somehow caught a glimpse of the future. A future in which only one of them would live to tell the tale.

WAR REPORT

Personnel: Ian Lowit, aka Hans Löwit, was born in Vienna, Austria, in 1919. He enrolled as a medical student at the University of Vienna. He left Vienna for Britain in 1938 after the Anschluss joined Austria with Nazi Germany. He worked in Scotland as a domestic servant, a trainee radiologist and a labourer before and after war was declared in 1939. In 1940 he was interned – imprisoned without trial – as an 'enemy alien'. He was held captive in Scotland, England and then Canada for two years. He was released and joined the British Army as an anti-tank gunner. He gave active service in Europe following D-Day in 1944. After the war he settled in Aberdeen to continue his training as a doctor and pursue a career in medicine. He settled down to marry and start a family, and became a consultant at the city's sick children's hospital.

Event Log: Internment of Enemy Aliens. Men living in Britain who originally came from countries that joined Nazi Germany's side once the war began were labelled as 'enemy aliens'. When western Europe fell to the Nazis in the late spring and early summer of 1940, there was a national panic that enemy aliens might try to help the Nazis conquer Britain. As a result, all male enemy aliens were arrested and interned. Since the start of the war, all those who were strongly suspected of having genuine Nazi sympathies had been locked up. The rest were eventually cleared of suspicion and released. Many joined the British forces to fight against the Nazis.

The Holocaust. This event was the mass murder of Jewish people, and other groups, in Europe, committed by the Nazis and their collaborators during the Second World War. The Nazis used the police, the army, government officials, and others, to identify and arrest Jews then transport them by train to pur-pose-built camps where it is estimated that more than 6 million died. Many were killed in specially built chambers filled with carbon monoxide gas or cyanide. More than one and a half million Jewish children were killed. The Holocaust is often described as 'genocide' – an attempt to wipe out an entire race of people.

Inventory: The Ordnance Quick-Firing 17-pounder heavy gun. This gun was mounted on a carriage and towed by a Crusader tank chassis. It fired shells that could pierce 13-cm-thick armour on a tank at a range of up to 1,000 metres. A crew of seven men was needed to operate the gun effectively.

CHAPTER 6
Fishing is a Blast

Cranes towered over the Glasgow fireboat as it made its way along the River Clyde. There were ships everywhere. Huge ships. Tiny ships. Some coming, some going and some staying put. There were old ships, new ships and not-yet-built ships. New vessels were being constructed in the docks at a furious pace, to replace the millions of tonnes of shipping sunk a few years previously during the Second World War.

On the deck of the fireboat was Sandy Ritchie, a veteran of the war and a former fisherman. As the fireboat approached its destination, Ritchie could observe fellow veterans working alongside older and younger men. These were the shipbuilders, swarming over teetering scaffolds and in shadows next to the looming hulls of tomorrow's latest cargo vessel or passenger ship.

Once upon a time many of these men had served in the fight against Hitler, as Ritchie had, dreaming of peace and prosperity. Now that the war was won, they each toiled away in their peacetime jobs, and many of their daydreams were of a pint of beer at the end of their shift, an eager welcome from their children when they got home, and a good view of the match on the football terrace at the weekend.

The sounds of shouting and whistling, of chugging engines, of curdling propellers, of horns, bells and whistles, all filled the air – as did more incendiary ingredients. There was the burning of coal, diesel, tar and cigarettes. There were the flames and sparks of blowtorches, as welders toiled to join together the huge plates of metal that would one day make a boat.

A stray spark or carelessly discarded cigarette butt would easily cause a fire. And so it was that on this occasion, as on many others, the crew of the fireboat had arrived at the scene of one such blaze, ready to douse it with thousands of litres of water extracted from the Clyde using a powerful onboard pump.

The fire had started in the interior of one of the ships under construction. It was now spreading and would have to be brought swiftly under control.

'It's burning through the deck!' shouted one of the young shipyard apprentices, clearly nervous and a bit frightened.

'Burning through the deck,' said Ritchie to himself. For just a moment he was lost in his own thoughts and memories.

Ritchie knew that he and his colleagues would soon have this fire under control. But he also remembered the nightmare of a hole burning through the deck of a ship he was once on many years before – during the darkest days of the war.

That ship was called HMT (meaning, His Majesty's Trawler) *Regardo*, a minesweeping trawler that patrolled the English Channel hunting for deadly naval mines – explosive devices laid in the water by the German Navy. The *Regardo* spent each night tied up in Portsmouth harbour with its crew on board in their bunks.

Every night more or less, the German Air Force – the Luftwaffe – dropped incendiary bombs on the harbour in air raids that kept Ritchie and his crewmates wide awake when they were supposed to be resting for the day ahead. The incendiary bombs were specially designed to start fires, and were made of a substance called phosphorus. It burned through anything – wood or metal.

The incendiaries fell down through the sky and landed on the deck of the *Regardo* with a rattle. Quick as a flash, Ritchie and the others used shovels to toss the fiery intruders over the side and into the water where they sizzled and sank. On one occasion, the head of one of these bombs got stuck in the wooden deck of the *Regardo* and the men had a highly stressful task trying to remove it before it burned a hole right through the ship and sank it.

For months, Ritchie and his crewmates never got any sleep. That was until eventually the commanders of the British mine-sweeping service realised that the men were too exhausted to work during the day. So it was decided that the minesweeping trawlers would have to spend the nights outside the harbour, in open water. It would be much harder for the German bombers to pinpoint them out there – and therefore the crew had a better chance of getting some rest.

Ritchie could remember an earlier time, when a good night's sleep was virtually guaranteed. That had been back at the start of his wartime career, when he and his fellow recruits were put up in a B&B to begin their training at a handsome and historic old fishing port called Lowestoft in East Anglia, on England's east coast.

Before arriving at the headquarters of the Royal Naval Reserve's minesweeping service in Lowestoft, Ritchie had been a teenaged fisherman living in a small village near Fraserburgh and working for his dad on a trawler in the North Sea. This is what Ritchie had done since he had left school. On the eve of the war, in the autumn of 1939, Ritchie and other lads with similar seafaring backgrounds were sent a telegram calling them up to join Britain's anticipated fight against Nazi Germany.

The authorities wanted these young fishermen's skills for the minesweeping service. As Ritchie discovered during his training at Lowestoft, this was because the minesweeping boats were converted fishing trawlers – and the way the minesweeping trawlers worked was in fact very similar to fishing trawlers.

By 1940 Ritchie had passed his naval training. He was sent to join the *Regardo*, a minesweeping trawler working in the English Channel, which is the stretch of shallow sea between Britain and France. The *Regardo* had, like the other boats, once been a fishing trawler but was now converted to military duties.

The vessel used a winch to reel out into the water a long wire with a serrated cutting edge. At the end of the wire was a buoyant device with a flag on it called an Oropesa float. This helped keep the end of the wire a safe distance away from the back of the trawler, and ensure that the wire was reeled far enough out to have a good chance of catching a mine.

The trawler also used other devices such as the box-shaped 'kite'. The kite dragged through the water and weighed the wire down to just the right depth to snare a mine. The way the system worked was strikingly similar to the way a fishing trawler held its net in the water to trap shoals of fish.

'We got another one!' shouted one of Ritchie's crewmates from the lookout platform next to the bridge. A huge, sinister-looking black globe with multiple horns protruding from its shiny skin had risen to the surface of the water. Despite its large size and weight, the object came up with such speed that it jumped slightly above the waves and then settled on the surface with a foamy splash.

This was a German naval mine. The enemy had moored it to the seabed using a cable attached to a weight, or sinker, where its job was to wait out of sight just below the surface until an unsuspecting British cargo ship brushed past it and then – BOOM! – it would explode, tearing a hole in the ship's hull, causing the vessel to sink and drowning the crew.

This mine was about to be denied its deadly chance. The *Regardo*'s cutting wire had broken it loose and brought it into view. Now Ritchie and his comrades worked to calibrate the trawler's big Oerlikon cannon mounted on the foredeck. The Oerlikon was an auto-cannon, a bit like a machine gun but much more powerful, and could also be used to defend the vessel from air attack.

Once the gun had been rotated and its barrel positioned so that the mine was in its sights, a safe distance from the ship, the order was given to fire. In an instant there was a blast from the gun, followed by a plume of spray from the sea, as the crew scored a direct hit on one of the horn-shaped detonators, and the mine was spectacularly destroyed.

The *Regardo* worked as part of a convoy that swept the

English Channel, travelling from Ramsgate, just north of Dover, then down and round the corner of England's southeast coast and westward to Portsmouth. This meant they swept for mines through the narrowest stretch of water between England and France, only about 20 miles wide in places.

It was a very busy and exceedingly dangerous place to be. There were convoys of friendly ships belonging to Britain and her Allies – but you had to keep your wits about you just to avoid a collision with any of these. Then there were the deadly E-Boats, which were vessels of the German Navy, the *Kriegsmarine*. Their job was to lay mines in the water, hoping to destroy as many Allied ships as possible and cut off vital supplies to Britain that would weaken the country's ability to fight against Germany.

Plus there was the Luftwaffe, or German bomber aircraft which took off from bases in Nazi-occupied Europe and menaced Ritchie and his comrades from the skies. During the night-time air raids the Luftwaffe dropped explosives and incendiaries. They also tried to machine-gun the minesweepers, forcing the crews to turn to the Air Ministry for help. Ritchie's boat was given a special, large air balloon, attached to the ship with a wire. The balloon floated in the air high above the *Regardo*, with the other ships moored next to it deploying balloons of their own. This didn't stop the bombs, but it did make it too dangerous for a Luftwaffe crew to fly in low and try to machine-gun the *Regardo*. The aeroplane would not risk becoming entangled in the wire and crashing into the water.

Each side was constantly thinking of ways to try to stay one step ahead of the other. As a result, the German mines were modified to make them more deadly. The mines were fitted with magnetic equipment. This meant that they could tell when the metal hull of a passing ship was close by, because the iron and steel used in ships was magnetic. When the ship came within blast range, the warhead in the mine was detonated.

Ritchie's vessel had to be fitted with a special bit of kit called degaussing gear, which made the *Regardo* neutral to magnetism – or 'amagnetic'. In other words, it would not attract a mine to its own hull. The crew still had to locate and deactivate the mine, though, and for this they used special electrical equipment of their own.

The *Regardo* sailed alongside two other ships, towing cables that put an electric current in the water. The electrical cables created a magnetic field that detonated the enemy mines. In order for the three ships to stay at a safe distance from the mines behind them, though, they all had to sail in an exact formation.

'Keep her dead abreast!' shouted the skipper to Ritchie, who was taking his turn at the controls in the wheelhouse. Dead abreast meant sailing with the bow of your vessel exactly in line with the bows of the ships next to you.

The *Regardo* used special lights that pulsed on and off to help Ritchie and the crew keep the boat in the correct position. But if you fell behind the others and a mine went up you would be blasted to smithereens.

The Germans, realizing that the *Regardo* and other British minesweepers were able to destroy the magnetic mines, took action. They added another new bit of kit to their mines, which was an acoustic head. It was operated by acoustics – meaning sound vibrations in the water – such as the sound made by a ship's engine. To neutralize these mines, the *Regardo* and other minesweepers were fitted with a special hammer that they used along with the electrical gear. One by one, they began destroying the acoustic mines too.

When not in their bunks getting a few hours' sleep between shifts, Ritchie and his crewmates worked day and night to try to make the Channel safer for Allied ships. But, despite their best efforts, sometimes things went terribly wrong. One of the *Regardo*'s responsibilities was to help sweep a Z-shaped channel between Portsmouth and the Isle of Wight just off England's south coast. So long as this channel was kept clear of mines, it gave a safe passage to other vessels. One morning, though, Ritchie and his crewmates saw the evidence of what happened when a ship strayed from the path.

'Look at all the letters floating in the water!' one of the *Regardo*'s crewmen shouted. The sea was littered with papers, wood and other debris. This was all that remained of the ferry which had journeyed early that morning between Portsmouth and the island. The crew of the *Regardo* had seen the huge explosion earlier, and feared the worst.

The ferry had left before the minesweepers went out, and had not correctly followed the Z-shape of the safe channel. As a result, the boat hit a minefield in shallow water and was completely destroyed. On board there had been many passengers, including young male and female service personnel who were returning home on leave. A large number of the crew and passengers were drowned.

Ritchie was reminded every day of how dangerous his life on the sea could be. He and his crewmates lost friends and comrades when one of their fellow minesweepers was sunk after it struck a mine during the night.

The *Regardo* itself came within a whisker of being blown up, too. It happened when Ritchie himself was at the wheel, steering the boat. While the crew were busy blowing mines, somehow the vessel ended up 'off station'. This meant it was not in the correct position.

If the men had been in any doubt about this, they soon got a violent reminder. A mine was set off during the sweep, but far too close for comfort. The blast was so strong it hurled Ritchie into the air, and his head hit the roof in the wheelhouse. The trawler's engine fared worse. It was knocked off its mountings leaving the vessel crippled. With the aid of another ship, the *Regardo* had to be towed in to the depot, but the crew knew they were lucky to be alive.

'You men have been in a hot corner for a while and we are very pleased with what you have achieved,' said the Commander at the depot back in Portsmouth. 'So I'm going to give you all a rest. You are going to the opposite corner of the British Isles – to Stornoway.'

Ritchie said goodbye to the *Regardo* and travelled to Glasgow. He found his new ship, which was another ex-fishing boat, on the Clyde. The name painted on the bow read *Dunraven Castle*, another of His Majesty's Trawlers.

'She's a nice boat,' said Ritchie to one of his crewmates, as he admired the vessel's design. The HMT *Dunraven Castle* was big, which was perhaps just as well because the crew were headed for the stormy waters of the North Atlantic and a stretch of sea called the Minches between the Scottish mainland and the Outer Hebrides, or Western Isles. The base for the area was in the port of Stornoway, which was the capital of the Western Isles on the northernmost, large island of Lewis.

'Our instructions are as follows,' said the Skipper, who had been a lawyer in London before the war. 'We are to sweep for mines in a southwesterly direction, starting up at the Atlantic side of the Orkney Islands then over to the Hebrides and down through the Minches, and right on down to Malin Head at the very northern tip of Ireland.'

It was the same journey up and down the Scottish coast that Viking invaders from across the North Sea had once made, except this time the invaders were the modern German *Kriegsmarine*. Each sweep of the area would take about a week and on Sunday nights the *Dunraven Castle* would tie up back at base in Stornoway, ready to begin all over again. During the week the vessel was moored at nights in whatever suitable lochs the crew could find on their travels.

Sometimes the crew would do a spot of fishing at night. This was not officially allowed, but since they were in a remote area the men knew nobody would report them. Besides, even their local superiors had very strange ideas about what official duties should consist of.

'We have a message here from the Commander in Stornoway,' said the Skipper one day.

The crew of the *Dunraven Castle* looked inquisitively at their Skipper.

'We are to transport fifty sheep from Stornoway across the Minch to Dunvegan.' Dunvegan was a pretty village with a historic castle and its own bay on the Isle of Skye, but herding sheep up the beach was not the crew's idea of useful active service.

Much more exciting was the occasion when they got orders to sail more than two thousand miles south in order to tow a floating dock from Britain to Gibraltar, in the Mediterranean. The floating dock was designed to be used to repair vessels where there were no proper shipyard facilities on land. At Gibraltar the structure was handed over to another vessel, which took it further on to Iran in the Middle East. Meanwhile, the *Dunraven Castle* made the return journey all the way up to its base in Stornoway.

Back in the Western Isles, there was plenty of serious work to be done besides the distractions of sheep and sly fishing. There were minefields to contend with. The British mined the waters in these areas to try to protect Allied convoys from the menace of U-Boats – the deadly submarines of the *Kriegsmarine*. The trouble was that, since the Northern and Western Isles could experience very stormy seas, these mines would often work themselves loose and drift dangerously into the path of friendly shipping – or even wash up in a harbour town and hit a seawall near civilian homes with potentially devastating consequences. So these stray mines had to be caught and neutralized.

When the crew of the *Dunraven Castle* were concentrating on hunting for mines, they had to be careful they didn't forget about the sea's other hazards. Though the Minches were not as much of a 'hot corner' as the English Channel, the area was far from quiet, with plenty of shipping traffic coming and going. On one occasion the minesweeper was sent out in a storm to the Butt of Lewis – the most northerly point of the Western Isles – to hunt for mines.

As the trawler heaved up and down and yawed from side to side in the heavy swell, and the crew busied themselves with their task, an Allied cruiser appeared and came charging down from the north without slowing down – and the *Dunraven Castle* was right in its path. Amid the wind, the rain and the wildly rolling sea, Ritchie and his crewmates had to keep their nerve as the cruiser steamed recklessly past and a collision was narrowly avoided. If the crew of a minesweeper had managed to avoid being blown up by a minefield only to be sawn in half by a passing ship, it would have been ironic.

Still, the threat of being killed by a mine was never far away. And never closer, in fact, than the occasion when Ritchie and three of his crewmates dragged a live mine down a beach with their bare hands. At the time, the *Dunraven Castle* was anchored at a place called Castlebay, the main village and bay on the island of Barra at the southern end of the Western Isles. The place took its name from the medieval stone castle built on an islet in the bay. Once upon a time the castle had defended the people of the island from attack by intruders in wooden galleys wielding swords and spears, but it was not much use against the state-of-the-art naval mine that was now lurking like a sea monster in the shallows between the rocks and the sandy beach.

To add to the stress of the situation, the *Dunraven Castle* had recently been assigned a mine-disposal expert. Having one of these specialists join your crew for a while meant you were certain to be assigned some extremely hazardous – or perhaps a better word would be suicidal – tasks. Here was one such task.

Following the instructions of the mine-disposal expert, who turned out to be a bit of a wild character, the men waited until the tide went out as far as it would go. The receding water carried the mine down the beach and away from the houses on the shore. Ritchie, along with the specialist and the two other crewmen, went ashore in a small boat. They carefully approached the mine and prepared to nudge it down into deeper water where it could be dealt with.

'After you!' said one of the crew to the specialist, who very gingerly but firmly began pushing the spiky globe through the water. The others joined in to lend a hand and they managed to wangle this live mine – which, had it gone off, would have torn them all to pieces – to a spot where it floated at a safe distance away from the shore.

'Now then,' said the specialist as he carefully unscrewed the horns of the metal beast, 'I have a question for you all.' As he kept the others in suspense he continued working methodically to deactivate the horns – the detonators that when pressed against a ship's hull caused the explosive powder inside the mine's belly to go off. 'Hands up,' he said finally 'who likes fish?'

Nobody was quite sure yet what was meant by this strange question – how many seafarers have you met who don't like fish? – but it would soon become clear. The lid of the mine was unscrewed and a lit match was dropped onto the powder, which blazed away in a controlled fashion. It was left to burn itself out safely while the landing party went back aboard the *Dunraven Castle*.

As the trawler rested at anchor in the harbour, and the mine smouldered away harmlessly in the background, thoughts began turning towards dinner. The hungry, growling bellies of the crew gave the specialist the obvious answer to his question and he promptly produced a mysterious-looking suitcase. He opened it and inside was a set of small detonators, intended for use in his work.

'Right, stand back,' he said to the others. They all looked on as he fiddled with one of the devices and then threw it overboard. There was a strange sound and then, after a time, there came bobbing up to the surface their evening meal – a dozen or so fish of various types, dead as doornails courtesy of an explosive charge from the mine specialist's box of tricks.

'A convenient way of fishing, wouldn't you agree?' he said.

Ritchie knew that soon he would face the prospect of fishing by more conventional means, using nets from a trawler based in some sleepy Scottish fishing village – but was that how he wanted to spend his life, once the war was over?

The end of the conflict was now in sight. By the end of 1944 the German forces were on the retreat, both at sea and on land. Ritchie was given a final posting to the Mediterranean to support Allied troops advancing north through Italy. His job was to help clear naval minefields laid by the Germans and the Italian Fascist government that had supported Hitler. Once these mines were neutralized, the sea could be opened up to civilian ships and some kind of normality could return to the continent as VE Day – or Victory in Europe Day – was declared on 8 May 1945.

A troopship carried Ritchie and hundreds of others back westwards to the French port of Marseilles. People could hardly contain their excitement and relief, with one fellow even climbing to the top of the mast to shout with joy while men down below rolled about on deck – all drunken sailors. Again, Ritchie thought, as the gangplank went down and he collected his things to board the waiting troop train that would take him back to the English Channel – what am I going to do now?

When he got back to Scotland his mind was soon made up. He tried to settle into the life of a civilian fisherman, but it was no good. Somehow the explosive life of a minesweeper had got into his blood and would not leave him. He longed for the excitement, the danger, the hustle and bustle, the flames, the sparks, the explosions – and the opportunity to combat these dangers and save lives.

The fireboat on the Clyde was waiting for him.

WAR REPORT

Personnel: Sandy Ritchie. As war broke out in 1939, young fisherman Alexander 'Sandy' Ritchie was called up from his home in Aberdeenshire for the Minesweeping Service. He was trained in Lowestoft, East Anglia, and then posted to the English Channel and an ex-Grimsby trawler called the HMT *Regardo*, now converted for minesweeping duty. The *Regardo* crew swept the channel for German mines between Ramsgate, near Dover, and Portsmouth. After a lengthy period in the Channel, Ritchie was posted to the HMT *Dunraven Castle*, based in Stornoway, with orders to sweep from Orkney in the Northern Isles to Malin Head in Ireland, passing through the Minches of the Outer Hebrides, or Western Isles.

Towards the end of the war Ritchie was re-posted again, this time to a minesweeper in the Mediterranean based at the island of Malta. Ritchie and his crewmates swept up the coast of Italy via Sicily, in support of Allied troops who were advancing north. When VE Day was declared in 1945, Ritchie's vessel had reached the port city of Civitavecchia, just north of Rome. After helping to make Italian waters safe for civilian ships, Ritchie was returned home and discharged from the service. He joined the marine division of the Glasgow Fire Brigade on board the Glasgow fireboat.

Event log: The Royal Naval Reserve ran minesweepers, anti-submarine vessels and other auxiliary ships for the Royal Navy. As the Second World War got under way, the Reserve became known as the Royal Naval Patrol Service (RNPS). Throughout the war, from the autumn of 1939 to the summer of 1945, the RNPS conducted a never-ending operation to keep the coasts of Britain clear of deadly naval mines so that Allied cargo ships and other vital vessels could safely reach their destinations and keep Britain's war effort going.

Inventory: The minesweeping trawler HMT *Regardo*. This ship had been a commercial fishing trawler before the war. When war broke out the vessel was requisitioned by the Admiralty – the government department in charge of Britain's Navy. When a piece of property such as a ship or building was 'requisitioned' it meant the owner was obliged to hand it over to the authorities, who sometimes paid the owner compensation.

Along with its minesweeping equipment, the *Regardo* was fitted with an Oerlikon cannon, a heavy rapid-fire gun that used explosive shells instead of bullets. The *Regardo* served throughout the war, eventually being returned to her commercial fishing owners in 1945. The HMT *Dunraven Castle* was also an ex-fishing trawler and it entered the minesweeping service in 1940. It was also returned in 1945. A requisitioned minesweeping trawler typically was powered by a three-cylinder triple-expansion steam engine.

CHAPTER 7
Escape from Home

The heavy cruiser HMS *Devonshire* was like a long, silvery sea monster with a back stickled by masts, funnels and gun turrets. As she steamed out of the open sea and into the Firth of Clyde, her captain made preparations for his final approach to the port of Greenock.

Under ordinary circumstances, a Royal Navy cruiser's successful voyage across the North Sea from Norway to Scotland would have been unremarkable. But these were not ordinary circumstances. It was June 1940. Europe was at war, and the *Devonshire* had come to within an inch of being torpedoed and sunk.

'Did you see that German plane circling over us?' said 17-year-old Reidar Torp to his father standing next to him on deck.

'Hmmm . . .?' said the teenager's father absent-mindedly, as the crew of the *Devonshire* tied her up and prepared to lower the gangway onto the pier. He was lost in his own thoughts.

As Torp junior would later discover, the plane had been a

reconnaissance aircraft of the Luftwaffe and it had taken a great interest in the *Devonshire* as she steamed away from the port of Tromsø in northern Norway, bound for Greenock. The plane's pilot had radioed to his base that he had spotted a juicy target, and his information was relayed to the German Navy – the *Kriegsmarine* – whose ships were dangerously close by.

'I swear I saw some explosions and smoke in the distance when we were at sea,' piped up a voice from the crowd as the *Devonshire*'s passengers disembarked and prepared to catch the train to Glasgow.

It turned out that during the *Devonshire*'s voyage, just a few nautical miles away from her, two German battleships had sunk a British aircraft carrier – HMS *Glorious*. The German vessels could have easily intercepted and claimed a further victim. But they didn't attack the *Devonshire*.

This, Torp heard later, was partly because one of the enemy ships was damaged. But, as Torp also discovered, the main reason may have been that the admiral in charge of the ships didn't trust anything he heard from the Luftwaffe – even though they were on the same side.

The captain of the *Devonshire*, on the other hand, dared not risk going on the offensive and attacking the German ships. The *Devonshire* would surely have been outgunned and probably sunk.

The battleships went back to Norway, which had recently been invaded and occupied by Nazi Germany, and in so doing they missed a golden opportunity. On board the *Devonshire* was the King of Norway, his son the Crown Prince, most members of the Norwegian government, and young Reidar Torp himself.

The passengers had made a great escape. The unlucky *Glorious* had been sunk because it was trying to evacuate British aircraft and more than a thousand personnel. For two months British forces had been trying to help the Norwegians push the invading Germans out of Norway. But, during this time, Hitler had decided to invade France, Belgium and Luxemburg as well. So the British decided to retreat from Norway to defend these other countries further south instead.

Many Norwegians accused the Allies – the British in particular – of betrayal. Yet just a couple of months previously the Norwegians had praised the British for helping them. As Torp settled down in his seat on the railway carriage bound for Glasgow, he reflected on how much things had changed in the past two months – and on his own story so far.

The afternoon of 8 April 1940 in Torp's home city of Oslo, the Norwegian capital, was an afternoon much like any other – except for the fact that a German invasion was imminent. Torp returned home from school and put a report he had written that day on the writing desk in his room.

He remembered thinking about his classmates. One of them was a Nazi sympathizer and was eager to see Hitler's army come up from Germany and conquer Norway. There were a lot of Nazi sympathizers in Oslo, but there were also a lot who were dead against Hitler – including himself and his father.

Torp's classmate didn't have to wait long. The following day, the German tanks rolled into Oslo and the city's glass shopfronts displayed big newspaper billboards declaring that Norway had fallen under Hitler's control.

The air-raid warning siren went off, signalling that an attack by the Luftwaffe was imminent, so Torp and his mother went down to shelter in the basement of their block of flats. When they entered the basement they were watched by some elderly ladies who were already inside. One of the elderly women spoke to the others in a voice that was deliberately high enough for Torp and his mother to hear. 'Well, I am glad that at least now we will get rid of the Norwegian government!'

This remark was aimed at the Torp family as though it were a weapon. Torp's father was at that time the Minister of Finance in the Norwegian government. This government was against the Nazis and Hitler, and dead against the German occupation of Norway. The woman was obviously a Nazi supporter.

Torp's father had already left home to take care of important business and make preparations for his family to be safely evacuated. The Germans were likely to take harsh action against the family of a Norwegian government minister who opposed Hitler.

When the moment came, the Torp family were packed and ready to leave Oslo. They fled first to Sweden, which was Norway's next-door neighbour. Then Finland, another neigh-bour. Then they re-entered Norway through northern Finland, high up in the Arctic Circle, where it was still icy and snowy even in April. When they got to the town of Tromsø on Norway's northwest coast, the *Devonshire* was waiting for them.

'Pretty amazing that this precious cargo made it here in one piece, eh Father?' said Torp to his father as they sat on the train and the Scottish countryside whizzed past. But his father wasn't listening. He was brooding over another precious cargo. He was thinking about the gold.

All the gold in Norway had been stored in a vault in Oslo, and it was crucial that it did not fall into Hitler's hands. It would have made the Nazis even stronger if they had taken it, and would have left Norway financially much weaker. So a plan was hatched to smuggle all of Norway's gold safely out of the country before the Germans got it.

On 9 April, the day the Germans came, Torp's father was in the Ministry of Finance playing his part in organizing the removal of the gold. While other government officials fled the capital, Torp senior stayed on in his office making calls.

'Are the trucks in place? . . . OK . . . uh-huh . . . very good, then.' He hung up.

Then the internal phone rang. It was the janitor, one of the last people still left in the building. 'Minister, the Germans have entered the main gate!' he said.

Torp senior locked the door, as beads of sweat formed on his forehead. He had to think quickly. He gathered his vital possessions together and then burst out of the door, down the corridor and through a warren of passages and doorways until eventually he made it out a quiet side entrance. The voices of German soldiers could be heard inside, barking orders and seaching high and low. Torp senior had managed to slip away with only moments to spare.

Meanwhile the trucks he had enquired about were put into action. The director of the Norwegian Central Bank had seen to it that trucks were lined up, ready and waiting to drive Norway's gold out of Oslo if the city fell to the Germans. The crates of precious metal had been loaded onto the trucks in secret and were on their way out of the country and onto a ship bound for Britain and then America – for safekeeping.

Just then, Torp senior's train of thought was broken and he was brought back to the here and now by an official passing through the carriage, checking the passengers' papers. They were almost in Glasgow.

'Are you ready, Reidar?' asked Torp senior. His son knew this was about more than just being ready to leave the train. The question was about how ready he was to do his bit for his country, by joining the Norwegian army.

Now that Norway was ruled by Nazis and their collaborators, the real Norwegian government and army – along with the royal family – had had to go into exile in Britain. They joined the British as Allies in the fight against Hitler across Europe, especially to free their homeland of Norway.

Torp junior joined the exiled Norwegian army in southern Scotland. He was drilled at a training camp north of Dumfries called Carronbridge, near Thornhill, and given the rank of corporal. A Norwegian Brigade was set up. To begin with, the men didn't even have any guns, but eventually some old, long-barrelled rifles were found for training. These weapons had been used during the First World War, but they still worked.

Torp was ordered to join the Norwegian Brigade Guard Troop, whose job was to guard the brigade headquarters. The headquarters moved from place to place during the war. One of the buildings it was based in was Brahan Castle, near Dingwall, in the north of Scotland, not far from the capital of the Highlands – Inverness.

A teenager who has just been made a corporal in the army during wartime has a weight of expectation on his shoulders. The question was, would Torp be up to the task? A chance for him to impress his superiors came when it was announced that Commander Strugstad, leader of the Norwegian Brigade, would be bringing the Norwegian Minister of Defence to Brahan Castle for a visit.

Torp climbed up to the top of the castle and positioned himself as lookout over the main gate, and organized his men in their positions. When the Commander and the Minister arrived, they were bound to be impressed that the young corporal and his platoon were on guard.

After waiting a while, however, the men grew restless and a little bored. They gathered around the young corporal to chat. As they talked and talked, they didn't notice the big car that was roaring up the road to the castle's back entrance. Suddenly, the car swept into the castle through the back route and caught the soldiers by surprise.

The minister was not impressed. He leaned across the car's leather seat and, in a loud voice, asked the Commander: 'Who is in charge of this platoon, Strugstad?'

The Commander cast a beady eye up at the uniformed figures hastily gathering themselves to attention on the ramparts and in the courtyard. He sniffed indignantly, and then leaned over and hissed in a very quiet, low voice: 'Your son, Minister. Your son!'

Torp senior had switched jobs from Minister of Finance to Minister of Defence. He would later enjoy telling the story of the day he caught his son off-guard. As for Strugstad, this was not the first time Torp junior had got into his bad books.

The other occasion followed a gas-mask drill down by the coast. Every Monday, Torp's platoon rehearsed how to cope with a chemical-weapons attack by putting on their gas masks and doing training exercises. At the end of the one-hour drill, Torp and his men were on their way back to their barracks when they were stopped by a Military Policeman, or MP.

'I want your men to do the drill again,' said the MP.

Torp, who was already tired, hungry and grumpy, was irritated by the MP ordering him about. 'Get lost!' he snapped.

Before he knew it, Torp was being marched to Strugstad's office at headquarters to face a punishment for insubordination.

The Commander looked at the young upstart standing to attention in front of him, then leaned over his desk and fixed Torp with his glare.

'Tell me, Corporal Torp,' began Strugstad, 'are you in charge here, or am I in charge?'

Torp considered this question carefully. His career in the Norwegian Army, and quite possibly his whole future, would depend on how he chose to answer. He looked at his Commander, and cleared his throat. 'You are, Sir!' he said.

'Right,' said the older man, a flicker of satisfaction showing on his still-angry face. 'Off you go then!'

Torp learned to show respect where it was due. He and his men sometimes left their barracks and went to village pubs, where they would play dominoes with elderly local men. 'Give the old men a good game but make sure you don't beat them,' said Torp to one of his comrades. 'Even though losing will cost you a pint!'

It was not all fun and games, however. There was plenty of work to be done. During the hard winter of 1942, Torp and his men spent many long days and nights digging snow to clear paths and roadways, and to rescue service personnel and civilians who were stuck. Sometimes they spent so long working out in the freezing cold in the middle of the night, up to their knees in snow, that when they returned to base to rest in the morning there were no food rations left for them – because other troops had eaten it all.

Snow also brought the chance for Torp and his platoon to train on skis in the Scottish hills. The skiing Norwegian soldiers had their pictures taken by war photographers, and one of these was even turned into a stamp after the war – showing Torp on a military training exercise, skiing down a Scottish hillside.

Being able to fight on skis could be a vital skill for the men in Torp's platoon who went on to join the 10th Inter-Allied Commandos. The commandos needed to be able to fight in any conditions. As it turned out, several of these men later took part in daring and dangerous missions against the German Army in Holland and other countries, winning a number of bloody battles.

There was another reason why being able to fight in deep snow, and on skis if necessary, was important. If a decision was made by the Allies to attack Nazi Germany by first invading snowy northern Norway, then the Norwegian Brigade would have to be ready to lead the invasion. As things turned out northern Norway was not invaded by the Allies – but the British and the Norwegians made a conspiracy to convince Hitler that it might have been. Hitler needed to be ready just in case, and kept a large number of German troops tied up in Norway instead of helping to defend France, where in the end the Allies decided to launch their real counter-attack.

This conspiracy, or deception plan, was given the codename Fortitude North. It was helped by a number of Norwegian spies who were recruited by the Germans in Oslo and flown over to Scotland in secret. Once in Scotland, these spies tricked the Germans by defecting to the British side and sending messages back to Hitler suggesting all sorts of fake British plans –

including that the Norwegian Brigade in Scotland was going to lead an Allied invasion of Norway.

The deception worked. Hitler kept more than 300,000 German troops in Norway when instead they should have been in France to help try to stop the Allies when they attacked on D-Day in 1944.

Meanwhile, a number of other brave Norwegians joined the resistance against German rule in Norway itself. This extremely dangrous work was assisted by a section of the Norwegian army, who were trained in Scotland, called *Kompani Linge*.

Among the men in *Kompani Linge* was Torp's cousin. After training in the Scottish hills, forests and seas, Torp's cousin and the other *Kompani Linge* fighters were sent to Norway, sometimes by a parachute jump from an aircraft, by boat, or else via neighbouring Sweden.

The *Kompani Linge* had two missions. Some of them worked for the SOE, or Special Operations Executive, conducting sabotage actions such as blowing up German ships in Norwegian harbours and things like that. The second group went into the hills and mountains of Norway and trained the people who had stayed behind. Torp's cousin was in the second group, and Torp himself was extremely proud when he learned about *Kompani Linge*'s work.

To prepare him for taking part in the fight ahead, Torp was sent to the Norwegian Military College in London and to Sandhurst Officer Training Academy in Surrey. By the time Torp's training was over, however, the Allies had advanced into Berlin, the German capital, and defeated Hitler. Norway was free again.

Torp caught a flight from St Andrews in Fife and returned to Oslo. It was almost five years exactly since he had left his homeland. Some things were just as he had left them, and other things were changed completely. In his room, his school report was untouched – just as he had left it – despite the fact the house had been used by a German family for years during the occupation.

One day Torp passed the Nazi sympathizer he remembered from his schooldays in the street. Torp stuck his nose in the air and made a point of ignoring the other man. Torp learned later, however, that his old classmate had had a change of heart. After the German invasion he had switched sides completely and became a supporter of the Allies and the effort to get rid of the Germans.

Torp's father and the rest of the government went back to running the country, and later his father was appointed the Prime Minister of Norway. Meanwhile, the gold that had been smuggled out was returned. Torp stayed in the Norwegian Army, where he worked to defend Norway's shores from attack by the Soviet Union during the Cold War. He rose to the rank of general.

Forty years later Torp visited Scotland to try to retrace his steps, looking for the young and strong-willed Norwegian corporal who had dug a lot of snow and done a lot of growing up during his wartime adventure in Scotland.

WAR REPORT

Personnel: Reidar Torp was born in 1922 in the town of Sarpsborg, south of Oslo, near Norway's coastal border with Sweden. In 1940 he was evacuated from Norway to Scotland on board

HMS *Devonshire* along with his family, the government and the
royal family. After serving in the Norwegian Brigade in the UK
he returned to his homeland in 1945. In the 1970s he became
the head of the intelligence, or spying, staff of the Norwegian
High Command. In the 1980s he was the director of the Norwegian National Defence College in Oslo and then director of
Norway's Resistance Museum until 1995.

Event Log: The Norwegian Campaign is the name for the battle
that was fought in Norway between April and June 1940, after
the country was invaded by Nazi Germany. The Norwegians
who did not support Hitler attempted to drive the Germans out
with the help of British, French and Polish forces. At first the
Norwegians were successful against the Germans but just when
it looked like the invaders might be forced to flee, the British and
French decided to retreat because their soldiers were needed
further south where Hitler's army had also invaded France,
Belgium and Holland. Norway was forced to surrender.

Norwegian resistance against the Nazis then split into two
parts. There were those who stayed in Norway and fought on the
home front against the Germans. Then there were those who
joined the Norwegian Army in exile in Britain, which spent
much of its time training and organizing itself in Scotland.
A number of soldiers in the army were trained to return to
Norway and help the resistance by launching sabotage
operations against the Germans, who stationed hundreds of
thousands of troops in the country in case of an Allied counter-
attack launched from Scotland. The sabotage operations were
very successful. In a combined effort that included the Red
Army of the Soviet Union, the Germans were eventually forced

to surrender Norway in 1945, at around the same time as VE Day was declared. It has been estimated that around 10,000 Norwegians died during the conflict.

Inventory: HMS *Devonshire* was a County-class Heavy Cruiser with a crew of almost 800. She was built in Plymouth. Her keel was laid down in 1926 and construction happened swiftly, with the vessel launching in 1927. During her wartime career the *Devonshire* was armed with a range of cannons, machine guns and torpedoes. She also carried a Supermarine Walrus seaplane, which was launched by catapult. The *Devonshire* sometimes served in the Indian Ocean and South Atlantic, but throughout the war she mainly served Norway. She sank enemy ships, protected Allied vessels and after the liberation of Norway in 1945 worked as a transport ship taking personnel home. After almost thirty years at sea, she was broken up at Christmas 1954 and sold for scrap.

Author's Note

The real-life stories in this book are based on first-hand inter-views conducted by the author. In narrating the facts of the subjects' reminiscences, some aspects of their stories, including some passages of dialogue and description, have been drama-tized. Any errors of fact or interpretation in what is presented here are the author's responsibility.

In addition to the original oral material gathered for this book, the author made use of a range of other sources. Some elements of the material presented here draw on an online archive exhibition created by the author for Museums Galleries Scotland and Aberdeenshire Council, entitled What's The War Got To Do With Us? – Remembering Scotland at War. The author would like to thank all those who supported and assisted him in that project.

In researching this book a range of published and unpublished works were consulted by the author, including *World War Two In Moray* by Bill Bartlam and Ian Keillar; *Duff House At War* by

Allan Burnett; *One Boy's War* by David Findlay Clark; *The King's Most Loyal Enemy Aliens* by Helen Fry; *Coastal Command 1939–42* by HMSO; *His Majesty's Minesweepers 1939–43* by HMSO; *John Moe – Double Agent* by Jan Moen; *Random Selection* by Willie Ritchie; and *German U-Boat Crews 1914–45* by Gordon Williamson. The author also consulted various online archives, including those of the RAF and the Imperial War Museum, and found valuable help the old-fashioned way from staff in archives including Glasgow Public Libraries and Norway's Resistance Museum in Oslo.